ASSESSMENT AND PROBLEM-BASED LEARNING IN THE LAW CURRICULUM

ASSESSMENT AND PROBLEM-BASED LEARNING IN THE LAW CURRICULUM

The PREPS Framework

Anil Balan

LONDON PUBLISHING PARTNERSHIP

Copyright © 2023 by Anil Balan

Published by London Publishing Partnership
www.londonpublishingpartnership.co.uk

All rights reserved

ISBN: 978-1-913019-94-5 (pbk)
ISBN: 978-1-913019-95-2 (ePDF)
ISBN: 978-1-913019-96-9 (ePUB)

A catalogue record for this book is available
from the British Library

Typeset in Adobe Garamond Pro by
T&T Productions Ltd, London
www.tandtproductions.com

Printed and bound in Great Britain
by Hobbs the Printers Ltd

Contents

Preface: introduction and rationale — vii

PART I: AUTHENTIC ASSESSMENT AND PBL IN LEGAL EDUCATION — 1

1. Background and context — 3
2. Vocational pedagogies — 15
3. Research design and methods — 25
4. Discussion of findings — 39

PART II: THE PREPS FRAMEWORK — 49

5. Preparing students for professional legal practice — 53
6. Building resilience and improving engagement for widening participation students — 75
7. Teacher and student adaptation to changing environments — 107
8. Responding to challenges of vocational pedagogies — 129
9. Integrating academic skills and vocational skills — 151

Conclusions and recommendations — 173

Notes — 179
Sources — 187

Preface: introduction and rationale

The priority given to skills development and employability by the relevant professional regulatory bodies for both higher education and legal practice has increased greatly in recent years. It is therefore timely to investigate the practical challenges brought about by the introduction of vocational pedagogies such as authentic assessment and problem-based learning (PBL) into the academic traditions of university law courses.

The impact of the employability agenda is perhaps felt most acutely at institutions such as my own former employer, the University of East London (UEL). At UEL I was the undergraduate course leader for law, and this was the primary institutional context for the empirical study that provides the foundation for this book – a study that was carried out in 2020 and 2021 as part of my doctoral thesis.[1]

UEL has a high population of students from 'widening participation backgrounds': this is a generic term used to signify students from non-traditional social, economic and ethnic backgrounds. Law teachers at UEL therefore face additional challenges in terms of teaching and assessing to meet the employability agenda, and with limited resources and less freedom, it is the ideal of a more rounded liberal education that suffers.

The incorporation of skills into law teaching is markedly different between 'new' (i.e. post-1992) institutions and older universities. A majority of the former expressly incorporate skills – such as drafting, interviewing, negotiation and communication – into dedicated modules or topics within modules; only a minority of the latter do this, and they are more likely to incorporate skills implicitly instead.[2] The literature also suggests that in new universities the student experience has been more centred on vocational preparation and that, in contrast to their peers in older universities, who had grown apart from legal practitioners, the commercial function of the law degree was perhaps more keenly felt at new universities.[3]

As a new university, UEL therefore teaches skills in a different way from the older universities, in that it is explicit rather than implicit in the curriculum, with specific modules, and topics within modules, devoted to skills teaching. The more established tradition of teaching professional legal skills explicitly at a new university and the greater familiarity of its staff with vocational approaches provided a strong justification for a study in this context. The impetus for this research therefore came in part from my own practical experience: that of a law teacher at an institution that is directly and heavily influenced by the employability agenda.

Part of the rationale for my empirical study was that the crucial perspective of law teachers on the challenges they face in teaching professional legal skills has not been given sufficient consideration. This is a significant gap, given that law teachers play a key role in effecting change within their institutions, and it suggests that the key findings of my research have the potential to have a major impact on legal skills teaching. A study that identifies how authentic teaching and assessment have been used previously, what challenges are faced and how these might be overcome also has wider significance for approaching legal skills teaching in the future. Specifically, the framework that emerged out of my study provides a set of guiding principles for incorporating authentic assessment and PBL into the law curriculum in order to prepare students for employment. These guiding principles are based on themes identified through empirical research: teaching for professional practice, teaching for resilience and engagement, teaching that adapts to the environment, teaching that responds to the challenges presented by vocational pedagogies, and teaching that integrates academic and vocational skills. I refer to these principles as the PREPS framework: shorthand for practice, resilience, environment, pedagogy and skills.

As I have already said, skills development and employability have become central aspects of legal education in recent years. This is because, as well as academic learning, students are increasingly expected to acquire training in reading, thinking, communicating and solving problems like a professional lawyer. This process mirrors developments in higher education more broadly, where the economic considerations of the value of an undergraduate degree have come to dominate debates about the quality of higher education. This is now such a prevalent way of thinking that the main educational purpose of a degree often now largely seems to be to prepare students for a future role in the workforce.

Following the mass expansion in higher education participation in the late 1980s and early 1990s, the issue of what key skills are relevant for employment (and throughout life) was the focus of the Dearing Report in 1997.[4] Dearing defined a set of generic skills to enhance graduate employability – including communication, literacy and numeracy, and problem-solving, team-working and IT skills – and he recommended that the provision of such skills should become a central aim for higher education. Reflecting the influence of the Dearing Report, employability is also now used as a benchmark for evaluating universities, increasingly being regarded as a priority by the relevant professional and regulatory bodies for UK higher education. By addressing the employability and skills development agenda, this book should thereby have a favourable impact upon many law students, not just those who will become legal practitioners.

For law in particular, the report that came out of the Legal Education and Training Review (LETR)[5] recommended that more emphasis on legal research skills, communication skills and writing for a range of purposes were desirable at all stages of legal education. Graduate employability is also a strong focus within both the Teaching Excellence Framework (TEF) and the Quality Assurance Agency's *Subject Benchmark Statement: Law*,[6] which identifies skills and attributes (as well as knowledge) as being key components of a law degree.

In 2015 the Solicitors' Regulation Authority (the professional regulatory body for solicitors) issued a new competency statement identifying the standards required for solicitors. It included using language appropriately and showing sensitivity when needed. The Solicitors Qualifying Examination (SQE) is a new centralized assessment designed to test whether students have met the standards set out in this statement. It launched in 2021, and the first assessments took place during the 2021/22 academic year. Adapting my own personal and institutional practices to address the challenges presented by the SQE, which has a strong focus on professional legal skills, is therefore a practical concern for me as well as a research interest.

These recent changes in the approach to qualification introduced by the professional and regulatory bodies create new challenges both for universities and for students in relation to the acquisition of legal skills and the extent to which these elements should be incorporated into law degrees. In particular, it can be argued that the SQE places a greater responsibility than ever before on university law schools to prepare law students for entry into the legal profession rather than leaving this to vocational training providers, as was the case previously. The overall drive seems to be to create a pervasive context within which professional skills are developed. This provides a strong justification for developing a framework for teaching legal skills in order to prepare students for employment.

Although student engagement is key to any employability-related curriculum reform, some commentators believe that law teachers hold the primary responsibility for effecting change.[7] Part of the rationale for this book was that the crucial perspective of law teachers towards teaching professional legal skills – and the challenges they might face in doing so – has not been given sufficient consideration.

An issue to consider in this context is the potential friction between a liberal approach to legal education and a vocational one, with the traditional focus of the former mainly on preparing law students to develop into better citizens and the main aim of the latter being preparation for professional practice. Again, this is a tension that is reflected in higher education more broadly, with the problematic move towards understanding the value of a degree in purely economic terms having already been noted.[8] If educational quality is linked solely to the earning potential of graduates after they leave university, this ignores the vital transformational impact of higher education in terms of shaping students' sense of who they are, what they can do in the world, and the role of extraneous factors such as social privilege and perceived institutional prestige on shaping educational and employment outcomes.

Law teachers are likely to encounter this tension mainly in the context of curriculum design, particularly in relation to assessment and in terms of how much time should be devoted to teaching skills such as writing, research and advocacy as opposed to black letter law, i.e. the technical content of law degrees. Traditionally, university law schools in the UK have focused on the latter, with the former being regarded more as the preserve of 'on-the-job' training, with the legal professional bodies using an apprenticeship model under which aspiring legal professionals learned in the workplace from experienced practitioners.

Only very recently has this traditional divide started to blur, and the change has brought with it particular problems for law teachers who wish to achieve the dual goals of encouraging deeper engagement among law students and contextualizing their classroom experiences. A central argument of this book is that skills – whether they are vocational ('soft' skills applied in practice, e.g. negotiation, advising, advocacy) or more traditionally academic ('hard' skills perceived as leading to the outcomes of a liberal legal education, e.g. reading, research, reasoning) – are mostly contextualized to their field of study rather than being wholly generic. Additionally, I argue that vocational pedagogies can potentially contextualize the development of legal skills and can help develop graduate attributes in the context of the discipline that is being studied. The use of the terms 'academic skills' and 'vocational skills', and even the distinction between the two, is recognized as problematic, however, and this will also be examined in this book.

The question, therefore, is not so much whether law programmes should increase the amount of legal skills teaching they provide, but rather how far-reaching this implementation should be in terms of curriculum and assessment design; the extent to which the most important stakeholders, such as law teachers, agree; and, ultimately, what approach this curriculum development should take. To address these issues, it is important to identify how teaching and assessment is being carried out at present, what challenges and opportunities are provided by current practices in this area, what needs to change, and how these changes are to be implemented, bearing in mind the practicalities that affect what interventions can be made, e.g. the effect of the coronavirus pandemic on face-to-face teaching (see below). Identifying and attempting to resolve these issues is a principal aim of this book, and I hope that addressing them will lead to wider implications for legal education in the context of the employability agenda, as well as recommendations for professional practice.

The ultimate aim of the study that provides the basis for this book was to develop a set of guidelines with a uniquely empirical basis: the PREPS framework, which is discussed in part II. This can be applied usefully by law teachers in the teaching of legal skills in order to prepare law students for employment by guiding the design of learning outcomes and assessment tasks in individual modules and throughout the law curriculum. As will be demonstrated in the chapters that follow, PBL and authentic assessment were the primary focus of my research because it is argued that assessment, both formative and summative, is an effective means of contextualizing employability skills in the curriculum, and authenticity is a key characteristic of assessment design that promotes employability. PBL and authentic assessment were therefore used in the study as lenses through which to examine the curriculum and the assessment design challenges that have been experienced in introducing vocational elements into academic courses.

Bearing in mind that the Covid-19 health crisis hit at the start of 2020, it is important to mention that the PREPS framework was developed in the context of an ongoing global pandemic. I was well aware that this might have an impact on not only the methodology of my study, but also its findings. I therefore anticipated some discussion of, for example, the shift to online teaching and assessment as a result of the pandemic, even if this was not the main focus of my research.

In just over three years, much has already been written about the effect of the pandemic on teaching and learning, both generally and in the context of legal education. It has been suggested that the challenging aspects of taking risks and making errors while learning to teach online seem to have been mitigated by a combination of more beneficial factors such as humility, empathy and even optimism among teachers. However, teachers have also said that transitioning online in the context of a pandemic distorts usual longitudinal perceptions of preparation and readiness.[9]

Something that has been widely discussed is the significant impact that the pandemic had in 2020 on graduate employment: for example, leading law firms deferred their graduate recruitment programmes; staff were asked to buy leave; and hiring, salary and promotion freezes were announced. It has been argued that "the repercussions of the Covid-19 pandemic may reverberate in the legal profession not only in the short and medium term, but for years to come".[10] This may result in greater expectations being placed on graduate employability skills, e.g. with regard to information and communications technology (ICT) proficiency, problem-solving skills and resilience. There might be practical difficulties in meeting these challenges, and that is something that this book will help to uncover.

*

The rest of this book is divided into two main parts. Part I covers the theoretical basis and the context for the PREPS framework, as well as looking at the methodology for my research (including the approach to analysis and a discussion of the main findings of the empirical study). The participants in the empirical study were law teachers teaching legal skills to students from widening participation backgrounds, and the study's findings therefore have particular relevance to widening participation institutions, which have tended to place a more explicit focus on legal skills teaching but which face additional challenges in terms of teaching and assessing to meet the employability agenda, with limited resources and less freedom. The findings of this research therefore have practical implications for the design of modules incorporating legal skills in the future, as well as being an original contribution to the literature in this field.

Part II is the main part of the book: it contains a detailed breakdown of the PREPS framework and how it can work in practice. This part can be read on its own, but part I does provide important background information for the framework. The PREPS framework can be usefully applied by law teachers to address the employability and skills development agenda within their institutions by guiding the design of module learning outcomes and classroom activities, and by helping with writing assessment tasks and criteria. An authentic teaching and assessment framework for legal education is particularly advantageous and timely given that, in light of wider developments in higher education and legal practice, law schools have become increasingly responsive to curriculum innovation in recent years as well as being more willing to try out new initiatives.

Rather than leading to major disruptive changes and interventions, the innovations proposed in this book can help to harness and build upon what may well already be taking place in law schools. As such, the potential impact of this book will be to allow the process of curriculum change within law schools to occur more smoothly than might otherwise be the case. The eventual effect of this transformation from within will hopefully be to enhance both the quality of teaching and the rigour of assessment of legal skills, thereby ultimately improving student performance and learning outcomes.

PART I

AUTHENTIC ASSESSMENT AND PBL IN LEGAL EDUCATION

This first part of the book will begin by examining the broad and contested concepts of employability, work-readiness and professional skills generally, before looking at them in the specific context of legal education and exploring inherent issues. In particular, we will look at the liberal/vocational divide: that is, the balance to be struck between the academic and vocational content of the law curriculum.

This part will also cover the meaning of key terms such as 'graduate attributes' and 'vocational pedagogy', and it will look at problem-based learning and authentic assessment as examples of the latter. In doing so, consideration will also be given to how these vocational pedagogies can be used as theoretical frameworks that are applicable to my research, in part by looking at the application of these concepts in previous studies.

Finally, I will use my review of the literature to develop research questions for constructing a framework for teaching legal skills in order to prepare students for employment.

CHAPTER 1

Background and context

EMPLOYABILITY, WORK-READINESS AND PROFESSIONAL SKILLS

While the term is open to a number of interpretations, employability can be defined as 'a set of achievements – skills, understandings and personal attributes – that makes graduates more likely to gain employment and be successful in their chosen occupations'.[1] This definition can be problematic though, as the concept of employability is widely acknowledged as contested, and there is no agreement on which skills and attributes are most likely to increase graduate employability.

The concept of employability is, however, generally used to describe student skills and attributes that make graduates more likely to find employment, such as problem solving, communication, self-management and team working. As such, the term 'employability' describes something different from whether students are ready to work in their chosen profession. There is therefore a need for some explanation of what 'work-readiness' means, as this is a term that relates to how prepared graduates are for the world of work rather than just their ability to find a job.

The term 'work-readiness' in this sense might simply be assumed to mean how well their education has prepared graduates to cope with their chosen profession from 'day 1' on the job. There is a developing view, however, that the skills that contribute to work-readiness should not be restricted to just field-specific knowledge and generic skills such as communication and reasoning skills, but that they should instead be extended to include personal attributes or intrapersonal factors, such as attitude, reflective skills, good personal presentation, honesty, integrity and respect for others.

Following on from this idea of an individual graduate's personal attributes being central to their readiness to work, it might be argued that at the heart of being work-ready is the concept of 'professionalism'. While this term is again tricky to define, it can be described as 'shared norms, high standards of competency and conduct and, importantly, a sense of public obligation'.[2] The universality and transferability inherent to the very nature of professionalism also seems important to emphasize in terms of the skills and values that any professional should posses. Professionalism is not, therefore, simply the rules of professional conduct as set out in a given jurisdiction: 'Professions involve (at least) a commitment to serve the interests of clients and the welfare of society.'[3]

It has been argued that the minimal requirements for a legal practitioner to be considered professionally responsible include the following: competence; clear, open and frequent communication with clients; and identifying, raising and discussing ethical issues.[4] Three further requirements can be added to augment this list: working in an autonomous way; exercising judgment; and having an ongoing commitment to lifelong education.[5] This need for continuing professional development is key, given that the body of professional knowledge required to practise will change continually. The importance of students developing the kind of self-monitoring skills required for lifelong learning has also been highlighted, and this seems particularly pertinent in relation to law students given that practising lawyers are obliged by their professional bodies to engage in continuous professional development throughout their careers.[6]

Professionalism should therefore not be construed narrowly as consisting simply of technical competence and adherence to the written rules of the profession. The term 'professionalism' can be regarded in a broader sense that places more emphasis on a number of universal skills, values and attitudes that guide an individual's behaviour and should therefore be an important focus for legal education. Professionalism therefore consists not only of field-specific knowledge, but also of skills and competencies.

However, 'skills' is another term that is not straightforward to define, since it also includes attributes that go beyond simply technical competence. There is a distinction between the academic or 'hard' skills traditionally associated with technical legal knowledge and with the intellectual qualities of a liberal legal education – understanding, analysis, critical thinking and legal research, for example, which law schools have tended to focus on in their curricula – and 'soft' skills applied in practice, which are designed to develop students' creativity, powers of persuasion and problem-solving abilities. These have not had the same prominence in the past. Vocational or 'soft' skills have been described as those that are both portable and valuable to any job or career. They may be either personal (concerning self-growth and self-management, e.g. resilience and persistence) or interpersonal (the ability to interact with others, e.g. teamwork, management and leadership skills).

In other words, there is a distinction between a lawyer's technical skills (you expect your solicitor to understand, analyse and be up to date on the law, for example) and their personal or interpersonal skills (you also expect your solicitor to be personable and to have a good working relationship with you). However, it should be recognized that there may an element of crossover between these skills as well, with there being obvious vocational value in academic skills such as reasoning, research, reading and analysis and clear academic benefits to students developing their resilience and management soft skills.

All of these skills are critically important for lawyers, and the incorporation of vocational skills at the undergraduate level of study enables students to learn early on that they need to focus on soft skills development as much as they do on the traditional hard skills of their chosen discipline. It is therefore appropriate for me to next give some consideration to the teaching of legal skills in the law curriculum in light of the concepts of employability, work-readiness, professionalism and skills described above. In addition, I will consider these contested terms further in the specific context of legal education.

TEACHING PROFESSIONAL SKILLS IN THE LAW CURRICULUM

It is first necessary to understand the place of professional legal skills teaching within legal education, with reference to the employability agenda.

The legal professional bodies associate professionalism with competence, e.g. in the form of the Statement of Solicitor Competence, which emphasizes core values, professional standards, individual morality and respect for community. The SQE tests whether students have met the standards set out in this statement by requiring them to apply their functioning legal knowledge to demonstrate the competences required of a newly qualified solicitor. The SQE assessment specification makes it clear that functioning legal knowledge refers to the depth and breadth of knowledge of law that candidates are required to demonstrate by reference to a range of core legal principles and rules that they should be able to apply to realistic client-based problems. It is significant that the Statement of Solicitor Competence takes a broad definition of competence as being 'the ability to perform the roles and tasks required by one's job to the expected standard'.[7]

The SQE also uses Miller's pyramid[8] – a model for the assessment of professional competence that is used extensively in other disciplines such as medical and dental training – to provide a framework for the assessment of solicitor competence. In assessing the application of the functioning legal knowledge required for effective practice, the SQE focuses particularly on the applied knowledge ('knows how') element of Miller's pyramid.[9] It is notable that the SQE, supplemented as it is by the Statement of Solicitor Competence, not only emphasizes technical legal practice (in the form of effectively undertaking legal research, drafting documents, undertaking advocacy and managing legal cases and transactions) but equally highlights the importance for lawyers of professionalism and judgment (including acting honestly and with integrity, maintaining competence and legal knowledge, and applying critical thinking to solve problems), of working with other people (by communicating clearly and maintaining effective professional relations) and of managing themselves and their own work (in terms of planning work activities efficiently, keeping good records and applying good business practices).

There seems to be a recognition, therefore, that professionalism goes beyond technical competence, and in a legal context it can include attributes such as 'autonomy, a fiduciary duty to the court and the ability to manage ambiguous problems, tolerate uncertainty and make decisions with limited information'.[10] The challenge for law schools is to mould the curriculum to the changing legal services landscape in order to produce employment-ready graduates by combining the learning of substantive legal content with the experience of practice. Employers are placing an increasing emphasis on recruiting graduates who have soft skills such as organization, team working and the whole range of communication skills (including language, articulation and presentation).

Outcomes-led curriculum planning is problematic, however, and there are problems with context-free statements of learning outcomes and with belief in 'transferable' skills.[11] Skills are mostly contextualized, therefore, and the capacity to discern the essential nature of a problem, decontextualize it and recognize the features in a novel context is a very high-level attribute. By way of example, both the technical or academic skills of a lawyer and the personal or interpersonal skills of a lawyer are contextualized: you expect your lawyer to be able to draft specific legal documents (such as advice letters); and the working relationship a client has with their lawyer is different from the relationship a customer has with their plumber or hairdresser, e.g. in terms of expectations of confidentiality.

This need for contextualization provides a sound justification for the incorporation of authentic teaching and assessment, as this could be a potential way of achieving the required outcome. It has been suggested that students find statements of graduate learning outcomes or attributes that are articulated at a whole-of-university level too generic to be meaningful, and that they are most likely to engage with learning outcomes that are contextualized to their courses and their personal situations, that are stated clearly by their teachers, and that are incorporated prominently into assessments.[12] Skills, whether hard or soft – and therefore, by extension, graduate attributes too – are thus not only highly context dependent but also need to be explicitly incorporated into the curriculum and assessed. Assessment in particular appears to be a logical focus for contextualizing employability skills in the curriculum, given that the tendency of students to prioritize learning associated with assessment is well known.[13] Authenticity has also been identified as a key characteristic of assessment design that promotes employability (see chapter 2), and it is clear that advice from employers, professionals and recent graduates, as well as exposure to industry-related experiences, can help make graduate capabilities more meaningful.

Designing assessment tasks to specifically assess the attributes and capabilities that graduates should acquire therefore seems sensible. However, contextualization of skills is not an easy proposition when it comes to designing the curriculum for law students and thinking about their assessment. As to how to actually achieve this in practical terms, one innovation that has been put forward for integrating graduate attributes into the curriculum proposes that learning activities for each professional field of study should be redesigned for each profession's workplace and perspective in order to ensure that work-ready understandings and skills are learned.[14] Active academic involvement in this process of developing and sharing learning activities and experiences is encouraged, as the importance of academic ownership of developing graduate attributes is regarded as key to the success of such curriculum renewal projects. Student attitudes may be equally significant here, since contextualizing their learning in terms of the profession in which they hope to gain employment could also help to dispel in students any impression that the content is not relevant.

What is actually meant by graduate attributes? Graduate attributes are referred to as being 'an articulation of the core learning outcomes of a university education',[15] and they are defined as the skills and qualities that extend beyond the disciplinary knowledge that graduates need to be capable of demonstrating for the changing needs of the modern workplace.[16]

As with other key concepts such as employability, work-readiness and skills, there is no one universally accepted definition of graduate attributes. However, referring to the following as attributes provides a useful starting point: written and oral communication, critical thinking, problem solving, information literacy, the capacity for independent thought and autonomous learning, and the ability to work in a collaborative and ethical manner.[17] Indeed, there is a great deal of consistency in the broad categories of desirable graduate attributes articulated in the literature, including both academic skills and what are often described as generic or soft skills. The attributes identified by professional bodies – including ethics and professionalism, a global perspective, communication capacity, ability to work well in a team and apply knowledge, and creative problem-solving and critical-thinking skills – are desirable for work-ready graduates precisely because, unlike technical skills, they are regarded as being too difficult for employers to instil in new graduates through training. However, a blunt 'checklist approach' to inculcating graduate attributes in students is undesirable due to the risk of fragmenting the curriculum and encouraging an overly rigid approach to teaching and learning.[18] This underlines the need for a clear strategy to support the development of skills in undergraduates.

Although higher education institutions have always placed importance on the desirability of developing these graduate attributes, for many students this has been an implicit consequence of their university experience rather than an explicit one.[19] What has changed in recent years is an increasing focus on incorporating graduate attributes in higher education curricula as specific additional learning outcomes in their own right, to be demonstrated through assessment as part of an outcomes-based approach. This pressure has been felt at a local level in UK law schools through reports such as the Legal Education and Training Review[20] and via UK-based quality assurance agencies (e.g. the QAA), but it is universal and has found its expression internationally through, for example, the Tuning Project in Europe and the Lumina Foundation in the United States.

To date, however, universities have struggled to integrate graduate attributes successfully into their curricula. This is hardly surprising, given that the assessment of graduate attributes is a complex and challenging undertaking, with difficulties including their translation into discipline-specific forms, the necessity to focus on course-level assessment, the maintenance of standards across courses, the complexity of tracking student progress in courses that permit diverse elective choices, resourcing implications and so on. In addition, if graduate attributes are not assessed, there is a risk that students and educators will not take them seriously, in spite of their importance both to government and to employers. This highlights a tension that is both central to this book and at the heart of legal education, and it again suggests a potential role for authentic teaching and assessment in relation to instilling graduate attributes and contextualizing legal skills.

THE LIBERAL/VOCATIONAL DIVIDE IN LEGAL EDUCATION

The extent to which a law degree can or, indeed, should develop the aforementioned skills, understandings and personal attributes is open to considerable debate, much of it centred on the balance between the academic and vocational content of the curriculum.

For many law teachers, considering the benefits and practicalities of embedding employability in their teaching, learning and assessment activities also involves thinking about how this approach can be reconciled with liberal ideals. A liberal legal education is traditionally thought of as being concerned with pursuing knowledge as an end in itself, and not necessarily as a way of preparing students for a particular profession.[21] This is a debate that goes to the heart of what legal education is for. Arguably, a liberal legal education would focus its attention on 'developing skills of knowledge acquisition through research, critical thought and debate'.[22] The vocational aspect of legal education, meanwhile, 'prepares students to apply their substantive and critical knowledge of the law to real-life situations … and equips them with the necessary skills to work with clients as legal professionals'.[23]

This traditional divide is partly due to the manner in which the academic law degree and the vocational training of lawyers developed in England and Wales, with professional bodies using a model of 'on-the-job' training for students to learn legal skills and undergraduate legal education having no formal role in preparing students for professional examinations. For example, this on-the-job training previously took the form of training contracts for trainee solicitors, where trainees learn from experienced lawyers over the course of two years– in a similar manner to an apprenticeship – before becoming newly qualified solicitors. This training contract was only embarked upon by law students after first passing a professional examination on completion of the one-year-long postgraduate Legal Practice Course (there is a broadly similar route to qualification for barristers). The university law degree was therefore focused more on the intellectual development of students, not on preparing them for a career in law, while preparation of students for entry into the legal profession was left to vocational training providers, e.g. the Law Society's College of Law (for solicitors taking the Legal Practice Course) and the Inns of Court (for barristers). The SQE does not formally bring university law schools into vocational training, but it may affect the ways in which they engage with it in terms of preparing students for this new professional examination.

While liberal education can perhaps be said to remain a priority for the majority of law teachers, it is also fair to say that most academics see no harm in a law degree having a vocational element in addition to the traditional academic study of substantive law. Indeed, for some this is a false dichotomy, since the professional value of the broad academic qualities associated with liberal education – such as understanding, analysis and critical thinking – should not be underestimated.[24] In this sense, it is possible for a liberal legal education to encompass vocational pedagogies that focus on preparation of lawyers for practice while also developing knowledge and skills for their own sake.

The term 'vocational pedagogy' has different meanings, which may reflect different educational traditions and influences. For example, it has been described as 'the science, art and craft of teaching and learning vocational education'.[25] This is perhaps not the best definition as it leads to a follow-up question of what 'vocational education' is, so the more straightforward description of vocational pedagogy as 'learning for work thereby developing the skills to labour effectively'[26] may be a better starting point.

Examples of the term in a legal context are also helpful in providing a clearer understanding of it. One example of a vocational pedagogy in law is clinical legal education (CLE), in which 'students are confronted with real client problems and work independently and collaboratively with peers and legally qualified supervisors to solve those problems'[27] in the context of a student law clinic, thus learning from practical, real-world experiences with the support of teachers and/or supervisors. Another example is experiential learning, which can be defined as education 'that makes conscious application of the students' experiences by integrating them into the curriculum',[28] and is thus again anchored in real-life experiences. It has been argued that the use of experiential learning can draw attention to the human and interpersonal dimensions of the law, and that it enhances contextual understanding. This advances liberal education in a manner that may be more effective than the more traditional essays, which can focus too much on legal doctrine, while ensuring academic rigour and helping students to develop their theoretical understanding.[29] Consideration of vocational approaches to professional skills teaching is therefore potentially instructive, and this topic will therefore be explored further in the next chapter.

Before that, though, it is important to first make it clear that the liberal/vocational divide is by no means unique to law teaching: very similar debates and changes have been taking place in other professional fields, such as education, health and engineering, for similar reasons. The growth of education-based vocational training has been referred to as being part of a state-sponsored strategy for the development of higher-level skills; as a substitute for on-the-job training by employers; and as a result of historic weaknesses in the provision of work-based education and training for young people in the English education and training system. In a series of seminars involving higher education professionals, Hodgson and Spours noted that while participants from the health sector recognized the value of vocational skills such as team working, those from engineering mentioned that it was harder to implement changes to established progression routes and traditional qualifications due to the strongly established community of practice within their sector.[30] This parallels to some extent what was said above about academic resistance to a vocational approach in legal education.

It should also be pointed out that vocational pedagogies in higher education have many similarities to the apprenticeship model of learning, which has been used in a wide range of occupations, from surgery to journalism, from cookery to music, and from hairdressing to fashion design. At its most basic level an apprenticeship involves a novice or trainee who is largely new to their discipline learning on-the-job from a highly skilled mentor or specialist, studying how to be morally upright citizens as well as acquiring occupational expertise in the process. Skill formation through a vocational approach to education has the potential to import many of the perceived advantages of the apprenticeship model: gaining disciplinary knowledge and the applied skills, values and processes of particular occupations in order to both mature as a person and grow into a professional identity. Vocational pedagogies can thus potentially contextualize legal skills development and help develop graduate attributes in context. How this can be achieved will be given further consideration by reference to two specific examples of vocational pedagogies with particular relevance to law.

The argument that legal education should not be purely vocational and that there is another purpose for higher education beyond simply preparing students for the world of work is compelling, and it can therefore be said that universities should indeed seek to prepare students for life beyond work, in accordance with liberal ideals. This is a proposition that most law teachers would probably find appealing, but this does not in any way suggest that they are thereby inherently opposed to adopting vocational approaches in legal education. Indeed, liberal legal education can embrace vocational pedagogies, both because of the professional value of the qualities most commonly associated with the former and because of the potential of the latter to contextualize legal skills and develop graduate attributes in context, preparing students for life as well as work in the process. The similarities between the apprenticeship model and vocational pedagogies is significant in this light given that the legal professional bodies have previously used a model of on-the-job training for students to learn legal skills. While for solicitors this traditional route to becoming fully qualified has now been replaced by the SQE, importing vocational pedagogies into the undergraduate law degree offers one way of retaining at least some of the advantages of the apprenticeship model in legal education and training.

CHAPTER 2

Vocational pedagogies

PROBLEM-BASED LEARNING AND AUTHENTIC ASSESSMENT AS EXAMPLES OF VOCATIONAL PEDAGOGIES

It is important from the outset to understand the theoretical basis for vocational approaches such as authentic assessment and PBL in order to establish a context for interrogating these approaches and their justifications.

Friction between focusing on the academic skills required for professional practice and on soft skills is mirrored in law curricula. Core modules stress academic skills that are customarily associated with the knowledge of law, including analysis, information gathering and legal research. However, more systematic incorporation of vocational skills modules – which enrich students' creativity, powers of persuasion and problem-solving capabilities – in law school curricula is necessary. Potential vocational approaches to this integration of hard and soft skills include the related concepts of problem-based learning (PBL) and authentic assessment. This book focuses on PBL and authentic assessment because of the potential to integrate different categories of skills successfully through their use and thereby instil crucial graduate attributes in context.

In PBL, students are presented with problems that are either real (that is, ones based on actual facts) or realistic (which may be taken from real life and adapted or be entirely fictional), and they learn by solving these problems and reflecting on the process of doing so. In 'authentic' learning settings, real-life authentic tasks are used to create the core of the learning environment, and assessment is therefore authentic where it replicates what students will be required to do in the workplace. We will examine the theoretical foundations for PBL and authentic assessment below.

PBL is a form of self-directed learning environment in which students learn through the experience of solving problems, working together in collaborative groups to identify both the factual issues and the gaps in their knowledge, applying what they learn and then reflecting on the whole process, with the role of the teacher being to facilitate this student learning. At the outset, PBL also requires articulating the learning outcomes of the task in terms of what teachers want students to know or be able to do as a result of participating.

PBL has a long history in other disciplines and it has been suggested that it is an approach that offers the potential both to help students develop flexible understanding and lifelong learning skills and to make students more effective self-directed lifelong learners and collaborators and more motivated learners.[1]

Authenticity is a key aspect of PBL. The learning comes from exposure to real or realistic work, usually based on an exercise that simulates a real-life encounter, but just as importantly it is frequently conducted in group sessions, with responsibility for learning and collaborating placed on students, who construct their own learning in the process. The key components of PBL for the purposes of this book are self-direction, group work and real or realistic problems with clearly defined learning goals, although the extent of this self-direction need not always be total.

While PBL is a model that could be regarded as an appealing alternative to more rigorously structured traditional learning experiences, some commentators have been critical of its self-directed nature. Some believe that the less guidance students are given, the less effective the learning is,[2] although these claims are – notably – not based on any empirical evidence that shows that more guidance given to students results in more effective learning. This criticism may perhaps be more relevant where the model of PBL is 'open' (i.e. where the student drives the process with little tutor guidance) rather than 'guided' (i.e. where tutors are more directive). This issue is considered further in the next chapter in the context of legal education.

Bearing in mind that PBL is an established teaching method in a number of other disciplines, it may be useful to note here lessons from some of those other contexts. In the health professions, for example, it has been noted that poor group dynamics may have a damaging effect on collaboration and communication, and that it is therefore important for group members to feel safe to explore and question knowledge.[3]

As an assessment-based extension of the teaching strategy of PBL, with which it has some similarities, authentic assessment includes activities designed to replicate the 'real world' by using realistic scenarios, authentic documentation and practice-based technology. Authentic activities are defined by the following characteristics.[4]

(1) The students describe the tasks needed to complete an activity, investigate complex activities over a sustained period of time, examine the tasks from different perspectives, collaborate and use a variety of resources, and then have the chance to reflect.

(2) The activities have real-world relevance, can be integrated and applied across different subject areas, are integrated seamlessly with assessment, create polished products that are valuable in their own right, and allow competing solutions and a diversity of outcomes.

The practicality of these requirements for authentic teaching and assessment does need to be considered, as they ask a lot of students, teachers and institutions of higher learning. The increased demands on students, the additional staff workload and the extra resources required for authentic activities to be carried out effectively mean that this is neither an easy nor a cheap strategy to adopt, and its advantages need to be seen to justify such investment.

Like PBL, however, authentic assessment is a common teaching strategy in other professional fields. In engineering education, for example, through clear demonstration of industry expectations in a marking scheme used in an assessment, authentic assessment was used successfully to motivate and support students in developing their professional competence.[5]

The aspect of 'real-world relevance', while equally intrinsic to authentic teaching and assessment, is also potentially problematic. For assessing the authenticity of a task the following questions can be put to course leaders, as suggested by McNamara.[6]

- Are students required to mimic professionals in the real world and complete tasks using resources similar to those in the workplace under realistic conditions?
- Do tasks produce valuable, polished products?
- Are higher-order thinking, reflection and self-assessment seamlessly integrated with tasks?
- Does the student collaborate with other stakeholders when completing the task?
- Does the student need to exercise judgment in determining subtasks of the main task?
- Do tasks produce novel or diverse responses?

This list of questions raises significant issues and indicates that there may be many challenges involved in implementing authentic assessment. How can students mimic professionals in the real world if they do not have live examples to learn from? Does this mean that practising legal professionals have to be involved in authentic activities? If so, how are they (or any other stakeholders with whom students are expected to collaborate) to be resourced and deployed?

Finally, two other factors have been identified as intrinsic to authentic learning and assessment: student engagement and the role of academic staff.[7] Again, these are not straightforward matters given that they imply greater demands on students and staff than might perhaps be expected of more traditional classroom activities. The literature shows that designing – and indeed identifying – authentic assessment is no easy task, and it needs to be looked at from the perspective of both students and law teachers, with self-direction, collaboration and real-world relevance being key aspects. This topic will be examined in more detail later in the book.

THE POTENTIAL VALUE OF PROBLEM-BASED LEARNING AND AUTHENTIC ASSESSMENT IN LEGAL EDUCATION

PBL is a methodology that is used at many medical schools but few law schools (the University of York is probably the best-known example of the latter), and the bulk of what has been written about PBL is not law based. Despite PBL being particularly relevant to law, given that collaborative problem solving is at the heart of legal practice, there has been minimal research related to it in legal education.

PBL harnesses prior knowledge and makes students the primary drivers of the learning process as they call on both preexisting and newly discovered knowledge in discussing a relevant problem. This process encourages students to inquire, research and appraise their findings.[8] More critically, there are challenges implicit in PBL from the perspectives of design, implementation, assessment and evaluation. Grimes bears this out by setting out ten detailed steps for PBL, from reading and clarifying the problem to checking to see if learning outcomes are met.[9] Ultimately, though, Grimes acknowledges the value in students seeing the client's problems from the perspective of all interested parties and notes that, as well as being an aspect of authentic assessment, experiential learning adds a valuable dimension to PBL. This is an aspect that it is useful to consider further.

Taking another lesson from the use of PBL in the health professions, challenges identified there have included lack of training and support for tutors, time constraints, and lack of student recognition, and all of these issues need to be addressed through support and ongoing training for tutors if PBL is to be implemented effectively.[10]

A study involving use of PBL in a legal context explored the development of students' writing skills through the use of a problem-based practice-oriented course.[11] This research identified that students did not always relate their experience of academic writing to the skills needed for writing in practice, perhaps because real-life tasks were not always included. The study concluded that a clearer framework was necessary. This underlines the need for law schools to explore fresh ideas to equip their students for legal practice and to develop guiding principles for teaching legal skills. In light of this study it is perhaps surprising that more has not been written specifically about PBL in a legal context, although this may be because this approach to study is not well understood in legal education and because the term PBL is broad and is not always implemented consistently. In light of the suggestion from the literature about the positive effects of PBL, however, more research is certainly needed to obtain conclusive evidence of the impact that PBL has on student learning, and this provides support for an empirical study in this context.

Authentic assessment has been around since the 1960s, but its potential in law – a field in which it could become very significant – has been largely unexplored. It is, though, viewed as an effective way of contextualizing the law and legal theory, and of ensuring that students have opportunities to develop the critical-thinking and problem-solving skills that are needed in professional situations. It is also viewed as a way of developing the cognitive and performance skills that graduates need to acquire.[12]

But authentic learning activities and assessment tasks also have the potential to go beyond simply teaching and testing skills and preparing students for employment: they can also raise student aspirations and increase their motivation through explicit demonstration of career alignment and through the relevance of curriculum activities.[13] In a legal context, for example, showing students that there is often no single right answer is the key to why authentic assessment is suited to doing more than simply adding to a student's knowledge. It is in this area of uncertainty and contingency – of a practice that can be prepared for but never wholly predicted – that authentic assessment is particularly beneficial.

Opportunities to interview and negotiate can also help to address the skills gaps in commercial awareness, legal research skills and communication identified in the Legal Education and Training Review. Importantly, small-group work has the potential to protect against dropout and encourages student engagement, although this clearly may not always be the case depending on the context.

The advantages of authentic teaching and assessment are not restricted to enhancing employability: they also provide an opportunity for a more holistic approach to learning, where students see law in its wider operational setting, including seeing legal problems from the perspectives of all interested parties. This is a methodology that has the potential, therefore, to serve the agendas both of employability and of awareness of substantive legal doctrine through a single integrated approach to teaching and assessment, regardless of whether the course of study is seen as academic or vocational.

In authentic learning environments, students can learn from errors that do not have the same consequences as they might have in the real world. Authentic assessment can also require students to engage with critical and sociolegal analysis: reflecting especially on the interaction between law and society, and the powers and interests implicit in that interaction, including how lawyers can serve public policy and wider interests. In this sense, authentic assessment has been described as a way of responding to some common criticisms of higher education, e.g. that students have difficulty applying the knowledge acquired in different academic contexts, and that recent graduates are considered by employers to be rigid, unprepared for employment and unable to adapt to the demands of working life. Authentic assessment can simultaneously address these concerns and enhance employability by providing opportunities for students to practise skills and competences that are valued in the workplace, such as problem solving, and to develop capabilities that are important to their future jobs, such as coping with uncertainty, working under pressure, thinking strategically and communicating with others.

It has also been suggested that the benefits of authentic assessment extend to improving metacognition, self-reflection and higher-order thinking skills.[14] The significance of metacognition to learning processes is that it stimulates a deep approach to learning, which encourages students to construct their own understanding of knowledge in their discipline rather than simply remembering enough to pass their examinations.

Reflection is an important aspect of this because, through ongoing monitoring of their own learning by students, metacognition establishes the value and importance of both critical reflection and self-evaluation for successful workplace performance, as well as personal development. Reflection is widely acknowledged as a means of enabling students to extend their learning experiences beyond the classroom through examining their past performance and then using this understanding to alter their future behaviour. A valuable aspect of authentic assessment is therefore the chance to get students actively involved in the application of principle to practice, and then to have them take that experience and deconstruct it in a reflective process. Law teachers may therefore wish to consider the use of reflection to perform authentic assessment activities given its relevance in professional settings, where the ability to evaluate and self-monitor tasks is critical to independent workplace performance.

CHALLENGES OF PBL AND AUTHENTIC ASSESSMENT

Having established the place of professional legal skills teaching in the context of the employability agenda and having identified potential approaches, it is useful to explore the inherent challenges of these approaches, their associated dilemmas and the possible resistance to them, as well as looking at the opportunities they provide.

At first glance, PBL and authentic assessment seem perfectly attuned not only to embedding the sorts of professional skills required to meet the aims of the employability agenda in modern law schools but also to instilling the qualities associated with liberal education valued by law teachers. However, the challenges of teaching and assessing students authentically are significant, and they are not always easily addressed.

A main criticism of PBL regards its limitations when it comes to self-directed learning, with less guidance perhaps resulting in less effective learning, and this same charge might be levelled, to some extent, against authentic teaching. Academic resistance from staff who feel that lectures and seminars in the traditional format are the best teaching environment for students and that 'written examinations are the "gold standard" in terms of academic rigour' is a hurdle that has been identified.[15] There are, however, varying degrees of resistance, and, depending on their views, staff may agree to complete, partial or limited integration of authentic teaching into their modules, depending on how they choose to teach and assess. Even when one can rely on full support from staff, considerable challenges remain in terms of curriculum and assessment design if it is accepted that students learn most effectively in an environment that is as close to real life as possible.

Achieving the goal of providing authentic assessment is therefore neither quick nor easy. There are a number of key points here.

Students need to simultaneously be provided with less guidance in the classroom than they might be used to, given the self-directed nature of these interventions, and more support outside of it to cope with this type of teaching method. Much of the onus for this will fall on law teachers, who might equally have little familiarity with authentic activities, perhaps especially if they have no background in legal practice and hence lack some of the experience necessary to simulate real-world experiences in the classroom.

Any interventions to increase the authenticity of teaching and assessing skills and competencies first require training and support for those who will be implementing the changes. The practicalities of doing so must be in doubt, with the demands on, and the scrutiny of, higher education providers currently being as great as they have ever been owing to increased media coverage and uncertainty over student recruitment due to the coronavirus pandemic – as an additional result of the pandemic, budgets and resources are under greater pressure than ever before.

Alongside a difference in approach is the need to update the content of law programmes, which also requires the support of academic colleagues – a challenge that may be an uphill task. However, this is an approach that is explicitly encouraged in the QAA *Subject Benchmark Statement: Law*, which lists among the qualities of a law graduate the following: 'Ability to apply knowledge and understanding to offer evidenced conclusions, addressing complex actual or hypothetical problems.'[16] There might therefore be a mismatch between the QAA requirements and the realities of curriculum development.

That innovation of this kind is essential to authentic assessment is also demonstrated by illustrations from other disciplines where it has been used. In tertiary science education, for example, it has been argued that institutions need to develop and support industry and community connections so that all academic staff are able to include this aspect of authenticity in order to effectively create authentic curricula and enhance students' understanding of viable future career paths.[17] This is an area that is therefore ripe for further investigation, and the approach taken to facilitate the necessary changes is discussed in the following chapters.

CHAPTER 3

Research design and methods

RESEARCH AIMS AND RESEARCH QUESTIONS

Investigating the practical challenges brought about by the introduction of a vocational pedagogy into the academic traditions of university law courses is the overall aim of this book. In order to better integrate vocational pedagogies into legal curricula and ultimately develop an authentic teaching and assessment framework for legal education, my empirical study focused on the following research questions.

(1) From the perspective of law teachers, how has authentic teaching and assessment been incorporated into the law curriculum (both in discrete legal skills modules and in other modules)?

(2) According to law teachers, what are the challenges of incorporating and implementing authentic teaching and assessment practices?

(3) How have (or might) law teachers overcome any challenges in adapting their modules to incorporate authentic teaching and assessment and in preparing students for employment?

In order to answer these questions, what needs to be determined is how far reaching the implementation of authentic teaching and assessment of skills has been in legal curricula, the extent to which the most important stakeholders such as law teachers agree, and ultimately what approach this curriculum development has taken. The valuable perspectives of law teachers on these issues are not well known, and that is the focus of the empirical aspect of this study. Using research methods such as interviews, which allow multiple perspectives to be acquired, and generating qualitative data (in the form of opinions, feelings and ideas, as captured in interview transcripts) holds the promise of exploring this subject in more detail and with greater authenticity than would be possible with a larger-scale study that relies on quantitative methods to explore the lived experiences of law teachers.

Because the sample size is too small, the design of an exploratory qualitative study such as this one does not generate data that can be statistically generalized to all law teachers. Instead, the aim of my research is to provide better insight into a method of teaching based on a detailed exploration of the experience of a few (i.e. no more than a dozen) participants. This research is therefore a qualitative investigation of the change process from the perspective of law teachers.

SAMPLING

The main context for this study was UEL, and its participants were primarily full-time, permanent staff involved in teaching and designing undergraduate law modules. To avoid having too narrow a focus and too limited a sample, from the outset it was intended that teaching staff in similar positions at peer institutions would also be interviewed to give a broader context to the research in terms of participant background and teaching experience. In this sense, all the participant teachers were informants: they have some years' teaching experience (i.e. they are all familiar with the academic traditions of law courses), but they are also now working (or have worked recently) on courses that have incorporated vocational pedagogies.

Purposive sampling was used to build up a sufficient sample to satisfy the needs of the project, guided by theory, so that enough information could be obtained to help in generating conceptual categories. At least a dozen subjects were sought, in keeping with the nature of this research as a small-scale qualitative study, while retaining a large enough sample size to answer the research questions, with numbers split between those from UEL and other institutions for this purpose. These other institutions were all London universities in UEL's peer group, in the sense that they occupied a comparable position in most league tables; they had a similar student body – one that derives largely from widening participation backgrounds; and they were all former polytechnics and primarily teaching-focused universities.

Law teachers from other widening participation institutions were selected purposively on the basis that the needs of this research, as noted in the book's preface, are best served by studying teachers who work in those contexts. Particular factors such as personal characteristics and social and economic inequalities tend to prejudice students from widening participation backgrounds, who might as a result find it harder to gain graduate employment,[1] and this was a useful prism through which to approach this study given its primary institutional context.

APPROACH TO ANALYSIS

Thematic analysis was used for the purpose of analysing the data generated for this research through interviews, as the intention was to find themes and perceptions arising from the data that could be developed into guidelines as part of a framework for teaching legal skills through PBL and authentic assessment. This technique involves defining the data you are analysing: firstly by coding (i.e. applying tags or labels to the raw data in such a way as to link bits of the data to an idea that relates to the analysis), and then by grouping the initial codes into a smaller number of themes that capture something of interest or importance in relation to your research question.

Thematic analysis was used for its flexibility and usefulness in identifying, analysing and reporting patterns within data from interview transcripts. Academic opinion supports the use of thematic analysis for exploratory studies, such as this one, and it is recognized as having certain advantages, such as providing a rich and detailed, yet complex, account of data.

Coding was a time-consuming process in itself, and it then took further thought and close reading to determine the themes to ensure they were distinctive, coherent and consistent. They then needed to be refined by continually revisiting the data. Coding is about more than just giving categories to data: it is also about conceptualizing that data, raising questions, providing provisional answers about the relationships among and within the data, and discovering the data.[2]

Following established guidelines, there were several stages in my thematic analysis of the data. First, I familiarized myself with the data, reading the journals and noting down initial ideas, and I then generated initial codes. Thematic coding analysis can be used inductively, but there is nothing to prevent starting the analysis with predetermined codes or themes arising from relevant literature.

Next, I collated the codes into a number of potential themes, which were again guided by academic opinion, theoretical frameworks and previous studies. In adopting this approach I was conscious that such pre-specification might bias me towards some aspects of the data, but it could equally be argued that prior engagement with the literature might enhance the analysis by sensitizing me to features of the data that could otherwise be missed.

The final phase of the analytical process involved exploring, describing, summarizing and interpreting patterns within the data.

ETHICAL CONSIDERATIONS

Every effort was made to ensure that this research followed the appropriate ethical guidelines, as set out in the British Educational Research Association guidance, by first obtaining clearance from a university research ethics committee before any data was generated.

An overarching issue is that having one's colleagues as subjects brings with it not just the immediacy of experiences that are worthy as data; it may also bring their expectation that they are regarded in a particular way, even compromising the integrity of that same data. There may be reluctance on the part of proposed participants to get involved, as this research comes at a cost to them, not just in relation to their time but also in respect of their exposure in talking about their teaching, in terms of any reputational risk that they may have felt in presenting the more challenging aspects of their teaching. It was therefore necessary to reassure colleagues about my independence as a researcher and about the confidentiality of the research, and to stress that, due to their anonymity, their careers would not suffer as a result of their participation.

I also needed to be aware of the dual nature of my role in this project – as both a lecturer at UEL and as a researcher – and of the resulting risk that my personal connection to the research might affect both my interpretation of the data and the validity of my findings. While there are clear practical advantages of insider research, in terms of intimate knowledge of the institution in which the study is taking place and access to participants, the disadvantages may be substantial, particularly with regard to maintaining objectivity, given my close contact with and knowledge of both the primary institutional context and my colleagues. The potential for respondent bias, as well as for subconscious bias on my part, must therefore be acknowledged, as must the difficulty of achieving fully informed consent and true anonymity. Some suggestions for negotiating the challenges of insider research, which I bore in mind in approaching this project, include trying to foresee likely conflicts and making a plan to deal with them; recording my responses; and, where possible, collaborating with colleagues from outside my home institution in order to maintain an objective stance as a researcher.[3]

Participants were reassured that their anonymity would be protected (e.g. by using pseudonyms in both data storage and reporting), that data would be stored securely (e.g. by using encryption for electronic data), that consent (including consent to record and store recordings) would be as fully informed as possible (e.g. by using an information leaflet and consent form), and that involvement was entirely voluntary and could be withdrawn at any time. Interviews were carried out sensitively, in a non-judgmental manner, respecting the rights of the interviewees at all times. Subjects were also able to exercise autonomy in these situations, e.g. by declining to answer interview questions and by withdrawing from the project at any time up until its end date, simply by telling me they wanted to do so.

Research participant interviews used voice over Internet Protocol (VoIP) technology (e.g. Microsoft Teams) to record voice and video across the internet via a synchronous (real-time) connection in light of the continuing Covid-19 health crisis. While VoIP technology provides the opportunity to contact participants in a safe, time-efficient and financially affordable manner, thus increasing the variety of sampling, it was also appreciated that its use affects the areas of rapport, non-verbal cues and ethics (in terms of security of access to data and protection of privacy). In this respect, Teams had advantages over less secure forms of VoIP, such as Zoom, as its use allowed all data, including both recordings and transcripts, to be stored securely on an encrypted university network. A further advantage of Teams was its automatic transcription function, which greatly aided both the speed and accuracy of the transcription process.

INTERVIEWS

Interviews took place following ethical approval and the granting of informed consent from the participants who had been approached. Interviews were semi-structured, and each lasted about thirty minutes.

Semi-structured interviews have the benefit of using a common structure and key questions while allowing the flexibility for unanticipated insights to be provided by interviewees and for interviewers to seek clarification, invite expansion or explore a response further. A schedule that had been fine-tuned through a pilot interview guided the interviews. The schedule covered

- how teachers taught and assessed legal skills in their modules,
- the ways in which teachers would like to enhance how they teach and assess legal skills,
- the specific aspects of legal-skills teaching and assessment practices that teachers feel have worked particularly well,
- what standard of work students produced in legal-skills assessment tasks for the modules taught by participants, and
- the challenges for both students and teachers of teaching and assessing legal skills.

Each interview was recorded using Teams and then transcribed, taking care to ensure that the written text reproduced exactly what the interviewees said, word-for-word, as far as possible. The transcription process was itself the first stage of analysis, as transcribing the interviews gave me an in-depth knowledge of the data, which was useful when refining themes for later analysis.

I have used pseudonyms for each interviewee (Ray, Nora, Rick, Andrew, Jack, Mike, Tracy, Derek, Justin, Carol, Bob, Laura) in order to preserve the confidentiality and anonymity of participants. I familiarized myself with the data collected through the transcription of the recorded files. Although this was an involved and time-consuming process, it helped me identify some ideas for potential themes. Since using memos to jot down possible thoughts about themes can be crucial in data processing, I also made notes about potential themes at this stage to use in the following phase.

In general, it was helpful to send the interview schedule to participants in advance, as this gave them an opportunity to consider the questions and think about their answers. Teams largely worked very well for interview purposes, with clear benefits in terms of safety, security and transcription. Most of the interviewees, though not all of them, were comfortable with video as well as audio capture of their interviews, and I found that it generally made no difference to the conduct of the interviews, either in terms of their length or the degree of rapport between interviewer and interviewee. If anything, the longest interviews were those that had no video element, perhaps indicating that at least some of the interviewees felt more comfortable with audio only.

All of the interviewees gave their longest answers to the first couple of questions, with the later answers tending to be shorter and more hesitant, either because the interviewees found them harder or perhaps because they became tired towards the end of the interview. This seems to bear out suggestions in the relevant literature that online interviews may in fact be more tiring than their in-person equivalents. There is a possibility of online interviews impacting negatively upon the areas of rapport and non-verbal cues, and this was borne out in this study in the sense that I felt I missed out on social contact with the other person to some extent, and on the energy that comes from that contact.

Throughout the interviews (particularly with those colleagues from UEL with whom I had worked for many years) I sometimes found it difficult to avoid the temptation to give my own views, especially when some of the interviewees asked me what I myself thought about something. This demonstrates a risk of insider research that is not often highlighted in the relevant literature: that of participants and researchers forgetting that they are in an interview and reverting to normal conversational behaviour. Nevertheless, I made a conscious effort to keep the interviewees focused, and the various prompts I had for interview questions (e.g. 'Can you give an example of that?' or 'Why do you think that?') helped considerably with this.

Participants were generally enthusiastic about being interviewed, and this was reflected in the depth and honesty of their answers. Indeed, colleagues often seemed to view the interview process as a useful opportunity to reflect upon their legal-skills teaching. Any direct quotes from the interview transcripts are presented without correction of spelling, punctuation or grammar for the sake of authenticity.

ANALYSIS OF DATA

The first stage of the analytical process involved transcribing the interviews, reading and rereading the data, and noting down initial ideas. I found it helpful at this stage to highlight any notable features that a participant had, or anything interesting about their answers to the interview questions.

All twelve of the law teachers I approached to participate in this study provided the requisite consent. Indeed, I was to some extent surprised by how willing – often eager, even – the participants were to be involved in the project.

The participants came from a broad range of backgrounds both within and outside UEL, representing a wide variety of modules at all levels. All but two of the participants were white. Eight of the participants were male, four were female. Again, all but two of the participants were very experienced lecturers, having ten or more years' experience in legal education. Six of the participants worked full time at UEL only, four worked both at UEL and part time at other higher education institutions, and the final two worked entirely at other institutions. Half of the participants were professionally qualified as either barristers or solicitors and had spent some time in legal practice; the other half were career academics who did not have professional practical experience but did have both relevant teaching qualifications (e.g. postgraduate certificates in higher education and/ or Higher Education Academy fellowship status) and expertise in teaching, designing and/or leading legal skills modules.

The interviews varied widely in terms of both the length and the content of the answers provided by the interviewees. I noted general features of the interviews and participants' answers, highlighting general points of interest, which were later revisited in developing codes and themes.

GENERATING INITIAL CODES

After familiarizing myself with the interviews through detailed reading of the transcripts, I made notes of what stood out in the data. In particular, I noted aspects that might form the basis of repeated patterns, such as specific events, activities and behaviours, i.e. what the law teachers did and said.

This part of the analysis involved organizing the data into meaningful groups, i.e. codes, which refer to the most basic segment, or element, of the raw data, or information that can be assessed in a meaningful way regarding the phenomenon. Since I was coding manually, I wrote notes on the texts I was examining and used highlighting to identify potential codes and themes. During this process I kept in mind both that it was necessary to code for as many potential themes as possible and that extracts of data needed to be coded inclusively to avoid losing the context in terms of the surrounding data.

Extracts from the data were given codes in a systematic fashion across the entire data set, with similar extracts being given the same code. The codes I chose were as follows.

- 'Technology': data concerning use of technology for legal skills teaching.
- 'Pandemic': anything related to the Covid-19 pandemic and its effects on legal skills teaching.

- 'Employability': where participants referred to how ready their students were for the workplace.
- 'Professionalism': discussions related to professional training, public speaking and use of legal language.
- 'Student engagement': where participants spoke about the difficulties of engaging their students.
- 'Widening participation': anything related to the challenges of teaching legal skills to students from widening participation backgrounds.
- 'Vocational skills': where participants discussed the sort of 'soft skills' required for legal practice.
- 'Academic skills': where participants discussed the sort of 'hard skills' traditionally associated with legal study.
- 'Authentic assessment': where participants talked about how they assessed students in an authentic manner.
- 'Problem-based learning': where participants talked about how they presented students with real or realistic problems.

All of these codes had sub-codes, and each code also linked in with the themes that were developed.

IDENTIFYING THEMES

In the next phase of the analysis I started to look through the data for themes – this is where the interpretative analysis of the data occurred. Codes were collated into potential themes; all data relevant to each potential theme was gathered; themes were checked to see if they worked in relation to the coded extracts and the entire data set; and, finally, initial codes and/or themes were revised if necessary.

From reviewing the literature I already had some themes in mind when doing the initial coding. Developing the themes out of the data involved organizing the various codes and thinking about how they could be merged to create an overall theme by searching for repetitions, transitions, commonalities, distinctions and so on. After coming up with an embryonic list of themes, the initial list needed to be reviewed in order to ensure that data within each theme corresponded closely with the theme, with clear and identifiable differences between them. At the end of this process, five themes were defined and named.

(1) *Preparing students for professional legal practice.* This was related to how work-ready students were in the specific sphere of the legal profession.

(2) *Building resilience and improving engagement for widening participation students.* This one focused mainly on the students and on the challenges faced by law teachers in relation to them.

(3) *Teacher and student adaptation to changing environments.* This theme was related mainly to external factors that impact on education.

(4) *Responding to challenges of vocational pedagogies.* This theme was based around how participants used authentic teaching and assessment.

(5) *Integrating academic and vocational skills.* Here, I was focusing both on the skills – soft and hard – that law teachers considered students needed to acquire and on the tension between them.

For ease of reference, the shorthand of PREPS – for practice, resilience, environment, pedagogy and skills – is used when referring to the themes.

MAKING COMPARISONS AND LOOKING FOR PATTERNS

The final stage of the thematic analysis process was in some ways both the hardest and the most crucial aspect of it. It involved finding and interpreting patterns and trends, noting the frequency of occurrence of recurrent events, making contrasts and comparisons between different aspects of the data, and attempting to make conceptual coherence within the themes developed.

One common thread among the participants was that legal skills – and the issue of how to teach and assess them – was increasingly becoming a focus in their teaching. This seems to reinforce the point made in the preface that skills development and employability are increasingly regarded as a priority by the relevant professional and regulatory bodies for UK legal education. I also found that while background, in terms of home teaching institution, was not a significant factor when it came to differences between the views that participants expressed in their interviews, professional background in the sense of whether participants had spent time in legal practice as opposed to academia alone did seem to have an impact on their answers.

So, while all participants, whether they were from UEL alone or had spent time partly or wholly in other institutions, tended to agree that the legal skills component of their teaching was increasing, there were key differences between them when it came to how this was happening and how authentic teaching and assessment were used to achieve this. For example, Derek, a career academic with no previous background in legal practice, chose to focus on critical thinking in the teaching of legal skills, while Justin, who came from a more practice-oriented background, spoke about legal skills teaching in terms of written and oral advocacy exercises. Further examples of these variations in approach demonstrated a consistent focus from those with practice experience on tasks that were more based on legal work, such as legal drafting and oral assessments, whereas those without time in practice tended to focus more on tasks that were more abstract (albeit ones that still have real-world relevance), such as problem questions and critical-thinking exercises. This was the case regardless of which institution they came from. More generally, this reflected the fact that in this study the answers of external participants were broadly consistent with those from UEL when it came to how skills were taught and some of the challenges in doing so.

In terms of looking for patterns within themes, I noted that some themes were more prevalent and harder to distinguish than others. So, for example, many participants spoke at length about the challenges of the ongoing Covid-19 pandemic and its effects in terms of moving teaching online, and these topics were captured mainly within the 'environment' theme and the 'technology' and 'pandemic' codes. However, this topic also had clear links with other themes such as the 'academic skills' and 'vocational skills' codes, and with 'pedagogy', made up of the 'authentic assessment' and 'problem-based leaning' codes.

For instance, Mike stated that the pandemic-initiated move to dual delivery presented technical and communications problems for both students and staff, and that it also impacted on the effectiveness of tasks involving collaboration. Rick said that there was lots of collaboration and group work in his seminars before the pandemic hit, but that he had found it difficult to replicate this during online classes.

Other themes were more discrete and crossed over less frequently with the others – most notably that of 'practice', which was made up of the 'employability' and 'professionalism' codes – while still being relevant to the overall thrust of the research in terms of identifying the practical challenges brought about by the introduction of a vocational pedagogy into the academic traditions of university law courses.

A significant trend that emerged from the themes I identified was that, when each participant referred to particular examples of their teaching and assessment practices that they individually felt were effective, these often crossed a number of themes. For example, Laura talked about how she had done a lot of work with students around essay writing skills, and the example she gave provided material for the themes of 'resilience', 'skills' and 'pedagogy', as she referred to the challenges experienced by widening participation students and how she addressed these through the use of both formative and summative assessment.

Other answers developed the literature in new and unexpected ways. Andrew, for example, helped to identify collaboration as a key feature of both authentic assessment and PBL, not just in the traditional sense of students working together in groups but also when it came to lecturers teaching together in teams. Again, this contributed to and developed the themes of both 'skills' and 'pedagogy'. These were among the most closely linked of the themes identified in my research, but each remained distinct and clearly defined in their own right.

Another common issue I identified was that participants made certain key points of relevance to this study that pervaded all the themes without necessarily being features of any of them in particular. Falling within this category was a point made by Mike that it could be argued that online teaching is every bit as authentic a learning environment as a physical simulation in the classroom, given that businesses in the real world are increasingly adopting online working practices. This potentially highlighted the authenticity of the use of online simulation by legal education providers, given that legal workplaces are similarly adapting to change by moving to online settings. Comments from Tracy when she questioned the very drive to teach legal skills and make students employment-ready and the motivations behind this at the policy-making level were similarly pervasive and significant. This also perhaps demonstrates both the benefits and the limitations of identifying themes as an analytical tool, and it emphasizes the importance of not viewing the themes identified in this study in isolation.

CHAPTER 4

Discussion of findings

I will now attempt to answer the three research questions that were posed in chapter 3 (see page 25). In doing so I will expand on some of the patterns identified through the thematic analysis process in order to highlight the main findings of my research.

LINKS BETWEEN THE 'SKILLS' AND 'PEDAGOGY' THEMES

Although the research questions were primarily about authentic teaching and assessment, the interview questions and the answers to them tended to focus on practical legal skills. Despite the fact that the term 'authentic assessment' was purposely not used in the interviews, there were examples in interviewees' answers of moving beyond identifying and teaching skills for employability and considering a vocational pedagogy of authentic assessment and elements of PBL.

The study findings that helped answer research question (1) tended to come under the 'skills' and 'pedagogy' themes, which seems to suggest that authentic teaching and assessment has been incorporated into the law curriculum, mainly in legal skills modules. There was plenty of evidence in the interviews of participants using authentic assessment and PBL for teaching legal skills in their modules, although this tended to take the form of formative assessment for vocational skills, with academic skills being assessed summatively and given more weight generally.

At its core, assessment is authentic where it replicates what students will be required to do in the workplace, and the key characteristics of authentic learning activities include real-world relevance, opportunities for students to collaborate and reflect, and tasks that can be approached from different perspectives and allow a variety of outcomes.

In this study, the examples of authentic teaching and assessment took the form of oral assessment, collaboration, group work and reflective tasks that possessed these characteristics: for example, use of oral presentations and legal drafting tasks in Rick's case; students working in teams to produce skeleton arguments for mock trials in Nora's case; and use of workshops to simulate practice environments in Carol's case. McNamara's questions (see page 18) were also helpful for determining authenticity in relation to specific tasks and activities when it came to asking, for example, whether students were required to mimic professionals in the real world and complete tasks using resources similar to those in the workplace under realistic conditions.

While the relevant literature was useful for identifying authentic characteristics of teaching and assessment, it was equally beneficial for highlighting the challenges of implementing authentic assessment that were subsequently brought out in this study. For instance, two of the factors identified as intrinsic to authentic teaching and assessment are student engagement and the role of academic staff. While there were indeed significant student-related factors, it was clear from my study that there were also major issues that law teachers struggled with when it came to implementing authentic assessment, and that they had varying degrees of success.

Often, there was a clear distinction between the processes used for authentic teaching and assessment and the intended outcomes from it. For example, Ray mentioned that he mainly taught legal skills by giving lectures, and that he used quizzes as a form of formative assessment, but he added:

> What you're trying to do obviously all the time is encouraging them to think ... so it's not such a big culture shock when they leave university from an academic background into the more practical background.

Ray's example here highlights a potential disconnect between teaching legal skills through, for instance, testing in a quiz and getting students to think like legal practitioners, which would need more authentic classroom experiences. This links back to a point made in chapter 2 when I referred to some of the literature that criticizes skills teaching that is decontextualized as being too generic to be meaningful to students, with a lack of engagement on the part of those students being a potential consequence of this.

This demarcation between outcomes and process was also notable from the fact that, while the traditional academic legal skills were familiar to participants and appeared well embedded in the legal curriculum, the vocational aspect had not yet been fully introduced and was to some extent still under development. This amply illustrates the point that achieving the goal of providing authentic assessment is neither cheap nor easy: lecturers face significant challenges in terms of having sufficient training, experience and resources to facilitate this teaching and learning strategy properly – something that was clearly borne out in the interviews.

To offset this, however, the advantages that law teachers spoke about also tied in closely with the literature. Authentic learning activities and assessment tasks have the potential to go beyond simply teaching and testing skills and preparing students for employment, as they can also raise student aspirations and motivation and help address skills gaps in legal education and training, such as commercial awareness, use of language and legal research skills.

The examples of authentic teaching and assessment that participants spoke about in their interviews included references to these benefits. In the example given by Nora of students producing skeleton arguments for mock trials, she referred to students not only getting valuable feedback to improve their work through this process but also having evidence of advocacy experience as a result, which would be useful for future legal work applications (especially for students who intended to practise as advocates). This could potentially have the additional beneficial effect of raising student aspirations and motivation. Similarly, in relation to Carol's workshops that simulated practice environments, she referred to the benefits as being not only to embed legal skills in everything students did but also to provide an environment that was more like a supervisor–trainee relationship than a traditional tutor–student one, thereby engaging students and preparing them for employment.

In view of these positive elements, striving towards authenticity in teaching and assessment therefore appears to be a worthwhile endeavour in spite of the evident challenges.

THE EFFECT OF PROFESSIONAL AND TEACHING BACKGROUND ON THE PERSPECTIVES OF PARTICIPANTS

My research suggests that incorporation of authentic teaching and assessment into the law curriculum seemed to be happening mainly at the level of discrete skills modules rather than as the result of a programme-level approach. This was apparent from the fact that participants tended to discuss innovations only in relation to the modules that they had thought about themselves rather than in response to any institution-led direction.

In one sense this might be viewed as concerning, given the necessity of maintaining standards across courses and focusing on course-level assessment in order to assess graduate attributes successfully. On the other hand, however, there appear to be benefits to this more individualized, module-level approach, which allows teaching and assessment to be tailored to personal teaching styles and subject-based requirements. Andrew, for example, specifically stated that how he taught and assessed legal skills depended on the module itself, with a practical subject such as clinical legal education being all about the application of legal skills through students taking part in mock trials and writing letters to clients, while for some of the more traditional modules, such as equity and trusts law, it was all about application of skills with regard to problem questions.

It was perhaps as a result of just such a module-level approach that different perspectives and divergences in approach were apparent among interviewees – largely dependent on their professional and teaching background – when it came to the teaching of legal skills. Most of the examples of authentic teaching and assessment that were provided were, notably, from the law teachers who had some experience of professional legal practice (e.g. Rick, Ray, Nora and Carol).

It was interesting that, when it came to the use of vocational pedagogies for the teaching of legal skills in their modules, staff who were career academics tended to make more use of PBL than authentic assessment. In PBL, students are presented with real or realistic problems and they learn by solving these problems and reflecting on the process of doing so. The tasks and activities identified in my study as possessing these key PBL characteristics of collaborative problem solving included the application of legal skills in problem questions in Andrew's case, problem scenarios that assess written skills and develop powers of reasoning in Jack's case, workshop-based discussions of legal topics in Mark's case, and legal referencing tasks and reading cases and statutes in Tracy's case.

Since most of these were examples of what has been described as 'guided' PBL – where tutors are more directive than they are in 'open' PBL – this at least partly avoided one of the main criticisms of this teaching and learning approach: that is, its self-directed nature, which was not suited to all students. At the same time, however, it has been argued that making students the primary drivers of the learning process is in fact one of the main advantages of PBL, so 'open' PBL perhaps has unexplored potential in this context.

THE IMPACT OF THE PANDEMIC AND OTHER ENVIRONMENTAL FACTORS

The most relevant findings of this study for the purposes of answering research question (2) came mainly under the 'environment' theme, with additional relevant points coming under 'skills' and 'pedagogy' when participants discussed the challenges they were facing that had perhaps led them to think about how they would enhance the way they taught and assessed legal skills. This uncovered unexpected challenges in incorporating and implementing authentic assessment and PBL. Rather than these challenges being based mainly on academic resistance to vocational pedagogies, the problems tended to focus more on students and their issues with, for example, adapting to more self-directed learning styles.

Equally unexpected was the effect of other challenges, such as the move to remote learning as a result of the coronavirus pandemic, as this involved law teachers adapting in ways that they were not traditionally used to doing. The concerns highlighted in the literature about risk-taking and making mistakes while learning to teach online as a result of the pandemic (as discussed in the preface of this book) were thus borne out when participants spoke about their experiences. For example, Rick and Mike both talked about struggling with the technological implications of the coronavirus pandemic when it came to using new equipment for teaching; Jack and Ray referred to the challenges of doing group work with students in online seminars; and Tracy mentioned sessions that had to be cancelled due to campus lockdown.

The impact of the pandemic was not entirely detrimental, however, as there were many examples of participants discussing its more beneficial effects and not just the disruption that was caused (this was partly reflected by the division of the 'pandemic' code into sub-codes relating not just to rapid change but also to future predictions). This also reflected the wider literature referred to in the preface, which mentioned the negative connotations of the coronavirus health crisis as being mitigated by a combination of more positive factors such as humility, empathy and even optimism among teachers.

In this study it was clear that, for some law teachers at least, the changes brought about by the pandemic ultimately led to them feeling that their legal skills teaching in fact more authentically reflected legal practice, through the use of technology in response to this external driver. Examples of this perspective were Jack's comments about moving into new territory more quickly and with less resistance in relation to changes to teaching, and Ray's reference to both teaching and professional practice increasingly moving online anyway and that trend only being accelerated by the pandemic. Some participants also mentioned inadvertent benefits for students caused by shift to online delivery. For example, Nora said that, despite students fearing that they would not get as good an experience, not being on campus and not being out and about all the time had actually made her students more focused in some ways, in that they were engaging more with formative assessment and sending in more work for feedback purposes.

THE CHALLENGES OF PREPARING STUDENTS FOR EMPLOYMENT

It is also significant that the sorts of challenge identified in this research were often related to preparing students for the world of work, and for legal careers in particular.

Although the main issues with implementing authentic teaching and assessment identified in the literature tend to relate to the challenges that teachers face, such as academic resistance to this approach, other difficulties relating to students have also been highlighted, and these were brought out further in this study. A common criticism of PBL relates to the limitations of self-directed learning, i.e. the less guidance there is, the less effective the learning is. It has been speculated that this criticism might also apply, to some extent, to authentic teaching and assessment, and, indeed, that student engagement is intrinsic to authentic assessment.[1] Ultimately, there were indications in my research that participants agreed with these views, to the extent that two codes relating to this issue of engaging and building resilience for students ('student engagement' and 'widening participation'), particularly those from widening participation backgrounds, were identified and combined to form the theme of 'resilience'.

This project was particularly useful for uncovering specific issues in relation to students from widening participation backgrounds who were studying legal skills – issues that did not feature as prominently in the literature. For example, Mike identified the challenge faced by students having to overcome their own anxiety regarding assessments; Laura spoke about the necessity for extensive study support, particularly for students with additional needs who required reasonable adjustments, covering basic skills taught outside the law curriculum, e.g. language skills; and Nora spoke about the additional demands this issue placed on lecturers because it was very labour intensive to introduce skills support in what she felt was the right way, which was within the curriculum and delivered by law lecturers in timetabled classes.

Other difficulties participants faced were conceptual as well as practical, For example, Laura queried whether there was at present sufficient time and space in the curriculum and in the academic calendar to consider whether the practice of legal skills teaching and assessment matched up to the theory underlying it, and she therefore questioned how authentic current legal educational practices actually were in reality.

Solutions to address lack of engagement in university life on the part of widening participation students have been suggested in the literature, such as encouraging disadvantaged students to participate fully in the non-academic aspects of university life,[2] but it was notable that participants in my study came up with their own innovative solutions, which potentially have wider implications for professional practice. For example, one method of tackling student disengagement that was considered to be effective by both Mike and Carol was to constantly reiterate to students the practical relevance of the legal skills they were teaching to them, while Laura adjusted her teaching and assessment to take account of individual students' strengths and areas for improvement and Tracy tried to provide more emotional support to her students. Although this arguably does not go far enough, as it is not the same as embedding skills in an authentic assessment, it is at least a useful starting point.

THE INCREASING FOCUS ON TEACHING LEGAL SKILLS

The answer to research question (3) takes the form of the PREPS framework (which is outlined in detail in part II). However, in developing the framework it is worth mentioning that it was the data linked to the 'practice' and 'resilience' themes that contributed the most useful material for how law teachers addressed challenges in adapting their modules to incorporate authentic assessment and PBL in order to prepare students for employment.

Participants in my study discussed interventions that they had used in the past, and they also included suggestions for approaches to take in the future. In many ways this research question was at the heart of the project, as the relevant data concerned issues pertinent to employability-related curriculum reform and, perhaps even more importantly, it would help to develop a set of pedagogical principles that are applicable to authentic assessment and PBL in law schools.

So, for example, where Tracy recommended a more holistic approach to the teaching of legal skills, by embedding them in substantive law modules, this suggested that it was better to teach vocational legal skills not in isolation but rather in combination with academic skills like legal reasoning. Bob also talked about the need for more integration of legal skills into core law modules in his interview. Authentic assessment potentially provides a means of doing this by relating the tasks that students do in the classroom to what legal professionals do in the world of practice.

It is possible to take this benefit even further as – at least from the perspective of the participants in my research – it seems to be the case that the more authentic law teachers can make tasks and assessments in terms of their resemblance to real-world legal cases, the more valuable they feel these experiences potentially are for developing legal skills in law students. This is illustrated by the fact that the enhancement to teaching and assessment that law teachers in this study talked about most consistently in their interviews was making classroom exercises and assessment tasks resemble practical real-life scenarios as closely as possible – whether that was in terms of exposing them to reading actual law reports, appearing in a working courtroom setting, or coming into contact with practising legal professionals.

But the advantages of authentic assessment and PBL are not limited to preparing students for employment: they can also extend to contextualizing the law and legal theory. Bob considered that this was very much the case in his collaborative legal skills workshops, for example, which focused not only on students reading, researching and writing international law together but also on those students reflecting upon and locating different sources of international law and thinking about possible topics for their final projects in groups. In his interview Derek talked about how he was thinking of introducing more formative oral assessment into the module, not only to give students practice at public speaking but also to help them learn how to summarize cases and to encourage them to collaborate in completing these tasks.

Integration of vocational and academic legal skills bears out some of the possibilities of authentic teaching and assessment discussed in the literature review as not only being restricted to enhancing employability. This sort of synthesis is also useful for increasing students' awareness of substantive legal doctrine and of law in its wider operational setting. Again, this is a benefit that can be taken further in that it could even be argued that, when integrating the teaching of legal skills into the law curriculum, some sort of synthesis with more traditional academic legal pedagogies actually seems to be key to the success of any vocational pedagogy. This was demonstrated time and time again in my study by the fact that tasks that seemed more focused on vocational skills development – such as oral assessment or collaborative problem solving – in fact had an invaluable role, in possessing elements of authentic assessment and PBL, in developing exactly the kind of academic legal skills that most law teachers would perhaps argue is an intrinsic benefit of the degree-level study of law at university. This is quite apart from the direct relevance of these skills to professional legal practice, whether in terms of critical thinking, legal reasoning, reflection, self-assessment, organization, professionalism or judgment.

PART II

THE PREPS FRAMEWORK

Thematic analysis was used in my empirical study to identify themes from the data, with the themes capturing features that were of interest or importance in relation to the research questions (see chapter 3). This analytical process produced five themes that cohered meaningfully with the data: teacher and student adaptation to changing environments, building resilience and improving engagement for widening participation students, preparing students for professional legal practice, integrating academic and vocational skills, and responding to challenges of vocational pedagogies.

The themes identified through this research not only provided a means of analysing and interpreting the data generated for my study, they also provided the basis of a framework for incorporating authentic assessment and PBL into the law curriculum in order to prepare students for employment. Thus, while the themes show what actually happened in the study and represent something important about the data, what I will discuss in this part of the book are principles that have been developed out of these themes – principles that contain practical proposals for future authentic teaching and assessment practices.

The guiding principles developed in this book bear some resemblance to the CARE framework,[1] but they have the advantage of being based on an empirical study designed for this purpose rather than being purely theoretical. What is more, they expand and modify some of the concepts identified in that earlier framework so that they apply in a legal education context, and they also take account of recent developments such as the introduction of the SQE. The CARE framework is a useful starting point, however, as it is perhaps the only previous attempt to develop a specific legal pedagogy for teaching (primarily soft) skills in law schools to prepare students for legal practice.

The CARE framework is a set of pedagogical principles based around compassionate, attentive, reason-based and empathetic teaching to help law teachers to enhance their legal skills teaching. Each of the CARE components represents both cognitive and emotional elements.

- Compassionate teaching prepares students for effective dispute resolution by minimizing conflict in the classroom, e.g. through use of the Socratic method (that is, the stimulation of critical thinking by argumentative dialogue).
- Attentive teaching involves teachers mastering the art of listening to their students, e.g. through feedback and encouraging classroom participation.
- Reason-based teaching aims to introduce legal reasoning to students, e.g. by considering legal case studies in groups.
- Empathetic teaching is about non-verbal communication between teachers and their students. It can take the form of collaborative work, mentoring or student law clinics.

There are shortcomings to the CARE framework, such as the heavy load it places on teachers and the difficulty of maintaining student motivation. However, the best way for law teachers to test the CARE principles in practice is to use them when teaching soft skills modules (and, more widely, throughout the legal curriculum). The actual implementation of the principles will depend on a number of factors, such as the level of both student engagement and participation of teaching staff.

The CARE framework can thus potentially be used as a starting point for guiding principles that are applicable to PBL and authentic assessment in law schools, as it is one of the only attempts thus far to develop pedagogical principles specific to law for teaching legal skills to law students to prepare them for legal practice. Adapting the

CARE framework to take account of PBL and authentic assessment might, therefore, help overcome some of the challenges of implementing these teaching methods.

Further gaps in – and links with – the CARE framework and the Statement of Solicitor Competence are highlighted later in arriving at my own set of principles for authentic assessment and PBL in legal education. For ease of reference these principles will be referred to as the PREPS framework, based as they are on the principles of teaching for professional *practice*, teaching for *resilience* and engagement, teaching that adapts to the *environment*, teaching to respond to challenges of vocational *pedagogies*, and teaching to integrate academic and vocational *skills*.

CHAPTER 5

Preparing students for professional legal practice

This theme was primarily related to industry-based factors, particularly in terms of how work-ready students were within the specific sphere of the legal profession. It emerged out of the data and partially reflected the thematic link between the 'employability' and 'professionalism' codes. The concept of work-readiness – in the sense of how ready students are to work in their chosen profession – was therefore important here, and this theme looks to builds on that concept. Again, there was some connection in the data between the two codes of 'employability' and 'professionalism', with the former more generally concerned with the role of legal skills teaching in readying students for employment and the latter focusing more narrowly on preparation for the legal profession.

Participants in my study seemed to have an awareness of the employability agenda and the policy drivers behind it, but this did not necessarily mean that they agreed with it or even felt that it was convincing. For instance, Laura mentioned that there was a great deal of enthusiasm for the use of 'mooting', or mock trials, for student assessment, but she expressed scepticism over the usefulness of incorporating such tasks into her sessions given their limited practical application. Similarly, while Tracy realized that in reality universities were judged on criteria such as graduate outcomes, there was for her an element of artificiality in the employment agenda in higher education institutions, given that in her view employers really wanted graduates that they employed to just do their jobs in the specific way employers wanted them done, regardless of whatever skills they were taught at university.

My study identified gaps in legal skills teaching when it came to preparing students for professional practice, especially in regard to more nebulous concepts such as commercial awareness and use of language (both Ray and Nora mentioned this in their interviews). The sub-codes of employability agenda, work-readiness, professional training, legal language and speaking skills that were identified within the codes of 'employability' and 'professionalism' helped identify these gaps – gaps that participants then focused on in their approach to authentic teaching and assessment.

Oral assessment and practising public speaking skills have important roles in encouraging deep learning and the development of higher cognitive skills. It is also worth mentioning in this context that the LETR highlighted the fact that opportunities to interview and negotiate can also help to address the skills gaps in commercial awareness, legal research skills and communication. Oral assessment, interviewing and negotiation exercises therefore seem to have great potential in relation to preparing students for legal practice. This builds upon the benefits mentioned in the literature, such as the potential of oral assessment for developing students' presentational skills.

In light of the discussion in chapter 2 about the importance of contextualizing legal skills, tailoring assessment to reflect the realities of legal practice may also have a crucial role to play in contextualizing legal skills for law students in their own specific professional context. Thus, despite the reservations and scepticism that Laura expressed, she took pains to incorporate oral assessment tasks that mirrored legal practice into her classes, e.g. when it came to students making oral presentations in front of their peers. Unlike written assessment tasks, however, these oral assessments tended to be formative rather than summative in nature.

As with the 'environment' theme, the 'practice' theme captures significant features of the data generated for this research. This theme also suggests a potential authentic teaching and assessment principle in relation to teaching that prepares students for professional practice that can be investigated in more detail when it comes to discussion of the implications and practical recommendations arising out of this study.

THE TEACHING FOR PROFESSIONAL PRACTICE PRINCIPLE

The principle of teaching for professional practice was developed out of the theme of preparing students for professional legal practice and from the separate individual codes on 'employability' and 'professionalism'. The preparing students for professional legal practice theme helped identify gaps in legal skills teaching when it came to preparing students for professional practice, especially in relation to concepts such as commercial awareness and the use of language, and it also identified the potential role of assessment tailored to reflect the realities of legal practice in contextualizing legal skills for law students. The 'employability' and 'professionalism' codes were divided into further sub-codes on professional training, legal language and speaking skills. This highlights the important role of oral assessment, interviewing and negotiation exercises in preparing students for legal practice, which participants focused on in their approach to authentic learning and assessment. The aspect of the CARE framework that accords most closely with the teaching for professional practice principle is 'compassionate teaching', with its emphasis on argumentative dialogue between teachers and students, but this lacks an explicit link with preparing students for practice.

Central to this principle is the idea of law teachers creating a supportive environment for students to develop their legal skills, in terms of both students building a rapport with their teachers and forming closer interpersonal relationships with their peers in order to increase their sense of belonging. There is therefore a link between this principle and the 'resilience' principle, where the importance of law teachers being both caring and attentive in building students' resilience (or their ability to cope) without damaging their confidence is emphasized.

An example of this aspect being brought out in my research was Laura's comments about the learning process sometimes being painful and students therefore needing time and space to practise (and be allowed to fail) at formative assessment before attempting any summative assessment.

The importance of relationships, communities and opportunities for failure in relation to developing resilience is well known. A recent large-scale study involved interviewing eighty students and staff from law and other disciplines to measure resilience.[1] The study concluded with some key recommendations for universities that are also relevant to this principle, particularly in relation to personal tutoring in terms of giving careful consideration to how personal tutors are selected and trained and also adopting a personal tutoring model that incorporates additional meetings. A case can also be made for resilience being a characteristic that is dependent not only on individual students but also on their surrounding circumstances. This emphasizes the potential for teachers to influence the resilience of their students by helping them to manage the challenges they face during their time at university.

The 'practice' principle also comes out of, and develops, the wider literature on authentic assessment. Authentic assessment should require students to carry out activities that reflect actual professional practices, and for performance-based assessment tasks students should be required to produce or demonstrate knowledge and skills in activities close to the profession.[2]

The teaching for professional practice principle therefore has significant implications for assessment design, as it suggests that, despite the difficulties of implementing assessments based around oral presentations, interviewing and negotiation (notably training staff and ensuring that they are adequately resourced), time and space need to be made for such assessments, and this includes formative assessment to prepare students during teaching. While the emphasis from participants in my study was primarily on oral tasks, written assessment also has a role to play in this context, and it has been suggested that appropriate forms of written authentic assessment could include case analysis, problem solving and essay questions.[3]

Given the relevance of this principle to professional practice, it is also important to ensure that assessments that prepare students for practice are as closely related to the actual practices of the legal profession as possible. One practical suggestion for ensuring this, and also for getting around the problem of staff not having the benefit of a professional background to help them design relevant assessments, is for them to collaborate with staff that do have such experience. The importance of law teachers who have significant experience and exposure to the various topic areas that they teach is regarded as critical,[4] which may be challenging where a law school lacks this sort of expertise in, for example, interviewing or other skills that might be central to a professional skills teaching module.

The PREPS framework can be linked back to the discussion of the SQE and graduate attributes in chapter 2, although each principle covers a number of different elements rather than mapping exactly onto just one requirement of 'The Statement of Solicitor Competence' (hereafter referred to simply as 'the Statement'). The practice principle, with its connections to employability and professionalism, most explicitly aligns with the technical legal practice requirement of the Statement by emphasizing practice-related skills like spoken and written advocacy and negotiating solutions to clients' issues. However, the professionalism and judgment requirement of the Statement mentions 'applying legal principles to factual issues, so as to produce a solution which best addresses a client's needs',[5] and the requirement of working with others refers to the need for candidates to demonstrate that they can communicate clearly and effectively both orally and in writing.

These requirements both also link in with the practice principle of the PREPS framework. When it comes to incorporating this principle into the curriculum, what appears to be important is for law teachers to create a comfortable and vibrant environment for students to develop their professional identities by practising their legal skills, exchanging ideas, resolving disputes and thereby preparing themselves for future roles as effective and eloquent conflict managers, with law teachers facilitating this development. This process is unlikely to be easy for either law teachers or students, as was made clear by participants in my study. For example, Rick spoke about how nervous his students were about oral presentations in particular.

However, the teaching for professional practice principle illustrates the potential, through authentic teaching and assessment, to develop essential graduate attributes by instilling in students skills that are universal and transferable, having relevance well beyond the discipline of law.

HOW THE TEACHING FOR PROFESSIONAL PRACTICE PRINCIPLE CAN WORK IN PRACTICE

The teaching for professional practice principle can be implemented in several ways to enhance the learning experience and prepare law students for professional legal practice. Some practical strategies that can be employed are listed below.

Authentic assessment

Authentic assessment is a powerful tool for evaluating students' understanding of legal concepts and their ability to apply them in real-world contexts. By designing assessments that closely mirror the challenges and tasks faced by legal professionals, educators can provide students with valuable opportunities to develop and showcase their skills.

One approach to authentic assessment is through oral presentations, which can simulate the experience of presenting arguments or legal analyses in a courtroom or professional setting. Students can be assigned topics or cases and asked to prepare and deliver persuasive presentations that demonstrate their ability to articulate legal reasoning and engage with critical issues. This assessment method not only assesses students' knowledge and communication skills but also helps them build confidence and public speaking abilities.

Interviewing simulations are another effective form of authentic assessment. Students can role play as lawyers or clients and engage in mock interviews, demonstrating their ability to gather relevant information, ask probing questions and provide legal advice or guidance. This assessment method helps students develop the crucial interpersonal and communication skills needed for client interaction in legal practice.

Negotiation exercises can also provide students with opportunities to engage in simulated negotiations, where they represent opposing parties and work towards reaching mutually beneficial agreements. These assessments require students to analyse the interests and objectives of each party, identify potential solutions, and effectively communicate and negotiate to achieve favourable outcomes. By participating in negotiation simulations, students can develop vital skills such as problem solving, collaboration and persuasive communication.

In addition, case analysis and problem-solving tasks can assess students' ability to apply legal principles to complex scenarios. Students are presented with authentic legal cases or scenarios and are required to analyse the facts, identify relevant legal issues and propose appropriate solutions or strategies. These assessments encourage critical thinking, legal research and the application of legal knowledge in practical contexts.

In addition to interactive assessments, traditional written assessments, such as essay questions, can also be designed to reflect real-world legal practices. For instance, students can be asked to draft legal memoranda, client letters, or legal opinions based on authentic case scenarios. These assessments can measure the ability of students to research and analyse legal issues, construct well-reasoned arguments and communicate effectively in writing. By incorporating authentic assessments into legal education, educators can bridge the gap between theory and practice. These assessments not only evaluate students' understanding of legal concepts but also provide them with valuable experiences that closely resemble the challenges they will face as legal professionals. Through authentic assessment, students can develop the necessary skills, knowledge and confidence to excel in their future careers.

Collaborations with professionals

Collaborations between law schools and professionals in the legal field can play a vital role in enriching the educational experience of students. By fostering these partnerships, law schools can provide students with valuable opportunities to connect with practising professionals, gain practical insights and develop a deeper understanding of the realities of legal practice.

One form of collaboration is through guest lectures, where professionals from various legal disciplines are invited to share their expertise, experiences and perspectives with students. These guest lectures can cover a wide range of topics, including specific areas of law, career advice, emerging trends and practical skills. By listening to professionals who are actively engaged in legal practice, students can gain valuable insights into the application of legal principles in real-world scenarios. Guest lectures also offer students the chance to ask questions, engage in discussions and network with professionals, expanding their professional connections and fostering a deeper understanding of the legal profession.

Mentoring programmes are another effective form of collaboration between law schools and professionals. Through these programmes, students are paired with experienced professionals who serve as mentors and provide guidance, support and career advice. Mentors can offer insights into the nuances of legal practice, help students navigate career choices and provide valuable feedback on professional development. Mentoring relationships allow students to develop professional networks, gain exposure to different practice areas, and receive personalized guidance that can shape their career paths.

Joint projects and case studies can also provide students with hands-on experiences and opportunities to collaborate directly with professionals. Law schools can partner with legal organizations, law firms or other institutions to design projects and case studies that require students to work on real legal issues or analyse actual cases. This collaborative approach allows students to apply their legal knowledge and skills in a practical context while receiving guidance and feedback from professionals. Through these projects, students can gain a deeper understanding of legal complexities, learn about ethical considerations and develop problem-solving and teamwork skills.

Collaborations with professionals can also benefit the legal community by fostering a culture of knowledge sharing and continuous learning. Engaging with law schools can help professionals stay connected with academic developments and contribute to legal education, and it can give them the opportunity to identify talented students for potential recruitment. These collaborations can also lead to research collaborations, joint conferences and other initiatives that advance both legal scholarship and practice.

In summary, collaborations between law schools and professionals in the legal field can provide students with invaluable insights, experiences and connections that complement their academic studies. Whether through guest lectures, mentoring programmes or joint projects, these collaborations can bridge the gap between theory and practice, they can enhance students' understanding of legal realities, and they can help shape students' future careers. By nurturing these partnerships, law schools can create a dynamic learning environment that prepares students for the challenges and opportunities of the legal profession.

Role playing and simulations

Role-playing activities and simulations are powerful tools in legal education that allow students to actively engage in realistic legal scenarios. By immersing themselves in these simulated environments, students can develop practical skills, enhance their problem-solving abilities, and gain confidence in their professional interactions.

One effective method is to incorporate mock trials, where students take on different roles – lawyers, witnesses, judges – to simulate courtroom proceedings. Through mock trials, students can apply their legal knowledge, develop persuasive advocacy skills and learn how to construct compelling arguments. They gain first-hand experience in examining witnesses, presenting evidence and engaging in legal reasoning, all within a controlled and supportive learning environment. Mock trials also encourage teamwork, as students collaborate to prepare their cases and present them effectively.

Client interviews are another important aspect of legal practice that can be simulated in the classroom. Students can participate in role-playing scenarios where they act as lawyers conducting interviews with clients. This allows them to practise effective communication, active listening and the ability to gather relevant information. By engaging in these simulations, students can learn how to build rapport, ask probing questions and provide clear and accurate legal advice. They can also develop skills in identifying clients' needs, managing their expectations and maintaining professionalism.

Negotiation exercises can also provide students with opportunities to develop their negotiation skills in a simulated setting. Students can engage in role-playing scenarios where they represent different parties in a legal dispute and work towards reaching a mutually beneficial agreement. These simulations require students to analyse legal issues, strategise and effectively communicate their positions. They learn to assess and balance the interests of their clients while engaging in principled negotiations. Through feedback and reflection, students can refine their negotiation techniques and understand the dynamics of resolving conflicts in a legal context.

Drafting legal documents is another critical skill that can be honed through role playing and simulations. Students can be tasked with preparing legal documents – such as contracts, pleadings or legal opinions – based on simulated scenarios. By engaging in these drafting exercises, students can learn how to apply legal principles, interpret relevant laws and communicate their analysis effectively in writing. They can develop an understanding of the structure, language and formatting requirements of legal documents, as well as honing their attention to detail and accuracy.

Incorporating role playing and simulations into legal education can provide a bridge between theory and practice. It can allow students to experience the complexities and challenges of legal practice in a safe and supportive environment. Through these activities, students can develop critical-thinking, problem-solving and decision-making skills that are essential for a successful legal career.

Role playing and simulations can also foster professional skills such as effective communication, teamwork and ethical considerations. To maximize the benefits of role playing and simulations, it is important to provide guidance, feedback and reflection opportunities for students. Facilitators or instructors can debrief the activities, provide constructive feedback and encourage students to reflect on their performance and areas for improvement. These discussions can enable students to gain insights into their strengths and weaknesses, enhance their self-awareness and refine their skills over time.

In summary, role-playing activities and simulations are valuable tools in legal education that can allow students to actively engage in realistic legal scenarios. Through mock trials, client interviews, negotiation exercises and drafting simulations, students can develop practical skills, enhance their problem-solving abilities and gain confidence in their professional interactions. By providing hands-on experiences within a supportive learning environment, role playing and simulations can contribute to the holistic development of students and prepare them for the challenges of legal practice.

Clinical programmes and experiential learning

Clinical programmes and experiential learning opportunities are essential components of legal education that can provide students with valuable real-world experiences and a deeper understanding of the legal profession. These programmes can offer students the chance to work directly with clients, under the supervision of experienced professionals, and they can bridge the gap between theory and practice. Clinical programmes can provide students with hands-on experience in a controlled and supportive environment. Students have the opportunity to work on actual legal cases, interact with clients and handle various aspects of legal representation. These programmes can be specialized, focusing on specific areas of law such as criminal defence, family law or immigration law, or they can be general in nature, providing students with exposure to a wide range of legal issues.

Internships can offer students the chance to gain practical experience by working in law firms, government agencies, non-profit organizations or corporate legal departments. These placements can allow students to observe and participate in the day-to-day activities of legal professionals, providing valuable insights into the realities of legal practice. Students may assist with legal research, draft documents, attend client meetings and even have the opportunity to argue motions in court under the supervision of their mentors.

Through clinical programmes and experiential learning, students can apply the legal knowledge they have acquired in the classroom to real cases and situations. They can learn how to analyse legal issues, conduct legal research and develop strategies to advocate for their clients. By working directly with clients, students can also develop essential client-management skills, such as interviewing, counselling and negotiation. They can learn to navigate complex ethical considerations and make informed decisions that uphold the principles of professionalism and integrity.

These programmes can provide students with exposure to the diverse challenges and perspectives they may encounter in their legal careers. They can learn to communicate effectively with clients from different backgrounds, understand their needs and tailor legal solutions accordingly. Through experiential learning, students can also develop problem-solving and critical-thinking skills as they navigate complex legal issues and seek innovative solutions.

Not only do clinical programmes and experiential learning opportunities benefit students, but they can also contribute to the broader legal community. Students may provide valuable legal services to underserved populations or assist in addressing social justice issues. They can contribute to the development of public policy, engage in community outreach and promote access to justice.

To ensure the effectiveness of clinical programmes and experiential learning, it is crucial to provide appropriate supervision, guidance and reflection opportunities. Faculty members, practitioners and mentors play a vital role in providing feedback and mentoring students throughout their experiential learning journey. Debriefing sessions, case discussions and reflective assignments can allow students to reflect on their experiences, identify areas for improvement and gain a deeper understanding of the ethical and practical dimensions of legal practice.

Ultimately, clinical programmes and experiential learning opportunities are arguably essential in legal education as they can provide students with practical experience, client interaction and exposure to the ethical and practical considerations of legal practice. These programmes can bridge the gap between theory and practice, allowing students to apply their legal knowledge, develop client-management skills and gain a deeper understanding of the legal profession. By participating in clinical programmes and experiential learning, students can better equip themselves to meet the challenges of the legal profession and to make meaningful contributions to the legal community.

Reflection and feedback

Reflection and feedback are critical components of effective legal education that promote student learning and professional growth. By encouraging students to reflect on their experiences and by providing them with timely and constructive feedback, educators can facilitate a deeper understanding of the complexities of legal practice while also helping students refine their skills. Reflection provides students with an opportunity to critically analyse their actions, thoughts and emotions in relation to their experiential learning and clinical experiences. It enables students to examine their decision-making processes, assess the effectiveness of their strategies and identify areas for improvement. Through reflection, students can gain insight into their strengths and weaknesses, develop self-awareness and cultivate a deeper understanding of the ethical and practical dimensions of legal practice.

Educators can facilitate reflection by incorporating structured reflection exercises into the curriculum. These exercises can take various forms, such as written reflections, group discussions or individual meetings with faculty mentors. Students are encouraged to consider their experiences, challenges and successes, and to explore the underlying principles and values that guide their decision making. By engaging in thoughtful reflection, students can develop a more nuanced understanding of the complexities of legal practice and cultivate a sense of professionalism and ethical responsibility.

In addition to reflection, timely and constructive feedback is crucial for students' professional growth. Faculty members, as well as peers and mentors, play a vital role in providing feedback that is specific, actionable and focused on both strengths and areas for improvement. Feedback can be provided through various means, including written comments, individual meetings and group discussions.

Feedback from faculty members offers students expert guidance and insights based on tutors' observations and assessment of students' performance. It helps students understand their progress, identify areas that require further development, and gain a clearer understanding of the expectations and standards of the legal profession. Constructive feedback not only highlights areas for improvement but also acknowledges students' achievements and reinforces positive behaviours and skills.

Peer evaluations can also be valuable sources of feedback because they provide a different perspective and promote collaboration and self-assessment. Peer feedback encourages students to engage in thoughtful assessments of their peers' work and provides opportunities for students to learn from each other's experiences. Through peer evaluations, students can develop their critical-thinking and communication skills while gaining insights into alternative approaches and perspectives.

To ensure the effectiveness of reflection and feedback, educators should create a supportive and inclusive learning environment. Students should feel comfortable sharing their thoughts, concerns and reflections without fear of judgment. Faculty members should establish open lines of communication and be approachable, creating opportunities for students to seek clarification, ask questions and discuss their progress.

In summary, reflection and feedback are integral to legal education as they can foster student learning, professional growth and the development of essential skills for legal practice. By encouraging students to reflect on their experiences and by providing them with timely and constructive feedback, educators can empower students to analyse their actions, identify areas for improvement and cultivate a deeper understanding of the complexities of legal practice. Through reflection and feedback, students can become more self-aware, they can develop a sense of professionalism, and they can refine their skills to meet the challenges of the legal profession.

Professional skills workshops

Professional skills workshops play a crucial role in legal education by offering targeted instruction and practice opportunities to help students develop proficiency in the essential skills required in legal practice. These workshops can focus on specific professional skills, such as legal research, legal writing, oral advocacy and negotiation, providing students with the necessary tools to excel in their future legal careers.

Legal research workshops can equip students with the knowledge and techniques needed to conduct comprehensive and effective legal research. Students can learn how to navigate legal databases, locate relevant sources of law, analyse and synthesize legal information, and apply research findings to specific legal issues. Through hands-on exercises and practical examples, students can gain confidence in their research abilities and develop the critical-thinking and analytical skills essential for legal practice.

In legal writing workshops, students can learn the principles of clear and persuasive legal writing. They can explore various types of legal documents, including memoranda, briefs and contracts, and they can learn how to structure arguments, cite authorities and communicate complex legal concepts concisely and effectively. Through writing exercises, feedback and revision, students can enhance their written communication skills and develop a strong foundation for drafting professional legal documents.

Oral advocacy workshops can focus on developing students' skills in presenting arguments and advocating for their clients in a courtroom setting. Through simulations, students can engage in mock trials or moot court exercises, where they argue legal issues before a judge or panel. These workshops can provide students with opportunities to refine their public-speaking, critical-thinking and persuasive-presentation skills. They can learn how to construct compelling arguments, respond to challenging questions and effectively communicate their clients' positions.

Negotiation workshops can introduce students to the art of negotiation and dispute resolution. Students can learn negotiation strategies, techniques for effective communication and skills for finding mutually beneficial solutions. Through role-playing exercises and simulations, students can practise negotiating in various legal contexts, such as settlement discussions, client interviews and business transactions. These workshops can help students develop their negotiation skills, including active listening, problem solving and building rapport, which are vital for successful legal practice.

To ensure the effectiveness of professional skills workshops, a combination of instruction, practice and feedback is essential. Workshops should be interactive, engaging students in hands-on activities, case studies and simulations to apply the skills they are learning. Faculty or practitioners with expertise in the specific skills being taught should lead the workshops, providing practical insights and real-world examples. Students should receive constructive feedback and guidance throughout the workshops to help them improve and refine their skills.

Moreover, professional skills workshops can be supplemented with resources such as online modules, tutorials or self-study materials that students can access at their convenience. These resources provide additional support and reinforcement, allowing students to continue developing their skills beyond the workshop sessions.

By offering professional skills workshops, law schools can ensure that students are well prepared to meet the demands of legal practice. These workshops can provide targeted instruction, practice opportunities and valuable feedback, enabling students to develop proficiency in essential skills such as legal research, legal writing, oral advocacy and negotiation. Through these workshops, students can gain the practical skills and confidence necessary to excel in their future legal careers and make a positive impact in the legal profession.

Integration across the curriculum

Integration across the curriculum is a fundamental approach in legal education that involves embedding practical components and skills development throughout the entire curriculum, rather than confining them to isolated courses or modules. By incorporating practical elements into substantive law courses, students can gain a deeper understanding of the practical implications of legal concepts and they can develop a more holistic approach to their legal education.

One way to achieve integration is by incorporating case studies, real-world examples and hypothetical scenarios into substantive law courses. Instead of focusing solely on theoretical principles, students are exposed to how these principles are applied in practical situations. By analysing and discussing actual cases or hypothetical scenarios, students can learn to apply legal concepts to complex factual situations, consider the implications and consequences of legal decisions, and develop critical-thinking and problem-solving skills.

Additionally, integrating practical components can involve incorporating drafting exercises, legal research assignments or simulated client interactions into substantive law courses. For example, in a contract law module, students could be assigned a drafting exercise in which they draft a contract based on a given set of facts and legal requirements. This would allow students not only to understand the legal principles but also to develop the skills needed to draft legally sound and comprehensive contracts.

Furthermore, integrating skills development can involve incorporating activities such as oral presentations, negotiation simulations and legal writing exercises within substantive law courses. For instance, in a commercial law module, students might engage in a negotiation simulation where they represent opposing parties in a commercial dispute. This would provide students with an opportunity to develop their negotiation skills, understand the dynamics of legal disputes and explore the practical implications of commercial law principles.

By integrating practical components and skill development across the curriculum, students are exposed to the practical application of legal concepts from the beginning of their legal education. This approach helps bridge the gap between theory and practice, allowing students to see the relevance and real-world implications of what they are learning. It also encourages students to think critically about legal issues, to consider multiple perspectives and to develop a well-rounded understanding of the law.

Moreover, integration across the curriculum promotes a more holistic approach to legal education by emphasizing the interconnectedness of legal principles and skills. Students can begin to see the connections between different areas of law and how skills such as legal research, writing and advocacy are applicable across various legal contexts. This integration fosters a more comprehensive understanding of the law and prepares students to navigate the complexities of legal practice.

To effectively implement integration across the curriculum, collaboration among faculty members is crucial. Faculty members from different areas of law can work together to identify opportunities for incorporating practical components and skills development within their respective courses. They can share best practices, develop common learning outcomes and ensure a coherent and coordinated approach to integrating practical elements throughout the curriculum.

Overall, integration across the curriculum is a transformative approach to legal education. By infusing practical components and skills development throughout substantive law courses, students can develop a deeper understanding of legal concepts, enhance their practical skills, and foster a more holistic and meaningful learning experience. This approach prepares students to thrive in the complex and dynamic world of legal practice, where the application of legal knowledge and the mastery of practical skills go hand in hand.

A supportive learning environment

Creating a supportive learning environment is essential in legal education. Doing so fosters a sense of belonging, encourages active student participation and facilitates the development of professional identities. A supportive and inclusive learning environment allows students to feel comfortable seeking guidance, asking questions and engaging in collaborative discussions. It also promotes open dialogue, respects diverse perspectives and provides opportunities for students to share their experiences and insights.

Faculty members can employ various strategies to establish a supportive learning environment. First and foremost, they can create a welcoming atmosphere by demonstrating approachability and openness. They can also encourage students to voice their opinions and participate actively in class discussions. They can emphasize that all perspectives are valuable and that respectful and constructive dialogue is essential for learning and growth. By setting this tone, faculty members can promote an environment in which students feel safe expressing their thoughts, challenging ideas and engaging in intellectual debates.

In addition, faculty members can create opportunities for collaborative learning, such as group projects, peer-to-peer feedback and interactive activities. Collaborative learning fosters a sense of community among students and encourages them to learn from one another. By working together, students can exchange ideas, share experiences and develop a deeper understanding of the given subject matter. Faculty members can facilitate these collaborative activities by providing clear guidelines, establishing group norms and offering guidance and support throughout the process.

Another important aspect of a supportive learning environment is the provision of individualized guidance and support to students. Faculty members can offer office hours, virtual meetings or other avenues for one-on-one interactions. This enables students to seek clarification, discuss their concerns and receive personalized feedback on their progress. By being accessible and responsive, faculty members can demonstrate their commitment to student success and create an environment in which students feel valued and supported.

Furthermore, faculty members can promote inclusivity by incorporating diverse perspectives and experiences into the curriculum. They can integrate case studies, readings and examples that reflect a wide range of cultural, social and legal contexts. This encourages students to appreciate the diversity within the legal profession, and it prepares them to navigate complex and multicultural legal settings. Faculty members can also facilitate discussions on social justice, equity and ethical considerations, creating opportunities for students to critically analyse the law's impact on marginalized communities and explore ways to promote equality and justice.

To nurture a supportive learning environment, faculty members can also encourage student-led initiatives and involvement in extra-curricular activities. This can include forming student organizations, participating in moot court competitions, organizing legal clinics or engaging in pro bono work. These opportunities allow students to apply their legal knowledge and skills in real-world contexts, to develop leadership abilities and to build professional networks. Faculty members can provide guidance, mentorship and resources to support these initiatives, and they can help students make the most of their experiential learning experiences.

Overall, a supportive learning environment in legal education is crucial for students' academic and professional growth. By fostering a culture of respect, inclusivity and collaboration, faculty members can create a space where students feel empowered to actively engage with the material they are presented with, to develop their professional identities and to build the skills necessary for success in the legal profession. This supportive environment not only enhances students' learning experiences but also prepares them to become ethical, empathetic and competent legal professionals who can contribute meaningfully to society.

SUMMARY OF KEY MESSAGES

The teaching for professional practice principle can work

- by incorporating authentic assessments that closely mirror real-world legal practices;
- by fostering partnerships between law schools and professionals in the legal field;
- by introducing role-playing activities and simulations that allow students to immerse themselves in realistic legal scenarios;
- by offering clinical programmes, placements and internships that provide students with opportunities to work directly with clients, under the supervision of experienced professionals;
- by encouraging students to reflect on their experiences and providing them with timely and constructive feedback;
- by offering workshops or training sessions focusing on specific professional skills, such as legal research, legal writing, oral advocacy and negotiation;
- by integrating practical components and skills development across the entire curriculum, rather than confining them to isolated courses or modules; and
- by fostering a supportive and inclusive learning environment in which students can feel comfortable seeking guidance, asking questions and engaging in collaborative discussions.

By implementing these strategies, law schools can effectively bridge the gap between theory and practice, equipping students with the necessary skills, knowledge and attributes to thrive in the legal profession. The teaching for professional practice principle ensures that graduates are not only well versed in legal theory but also possess the practical skills, professional judgment and ethical awareness essential for success in their future legal careers.

To ensure the successful implementation of the teaching for professional practice principle, however, and to maximize its effectiveness in preparing students for professional legal practice, it is important to address the following potential difficulties.

> HINTS AND TIPS
>
> » *Lack of practical experience.* One potential flaw of the principle is the challenge faced by law teachers who may not have significant professional experience in the specific areas they are teaching. Without practical experience, it can be difficult for law teachers to design assessments and provide guidance that accurately reflects the realities of legal practice, so it may sometimes be necessary for them to work with colleagues and others who do have a professional background and experience.
> » *Resource limitations.* Implementing authentic assessments, such as oral presentations, interviewing and negotiation exercises, can be resource intensive. Additional training and extra resources for staff may be required in order to effectively carry out these assessments, which can pose challenges for institutions with limited resources.
> » *Variability in student readiness.* The teaching for professional practice principle mentions the importance of formative assessment to prepare students during teaching. However, students may have different levels with certain professional skills. Some students may feel anxious or lack confidence when it comes to oral presentations or other practice-related activities, making it challenging for teachers to create a uniform learning experience. This must be borne in mind in the classroom.
> » *Assessing the breadth of legal practice.* Legal practice encompasses a wide range of areas, and it can be challenging to design assessments that cover the breadth of practice adequately. Assessments may need to be tailored to specific areas of practice, which can pose difficulties in ensuring a comprehensive assessment of students' preparedness for professional practice.
> » *Collaborative challenges.* Collaboration between law teachers and staff with professional experience is a practical solution to some of these other challenges. However, coordinating and facilitating

collaboration between individuals with different backgrounds and schedules can be challenging, particularly in institutions where such expertise is limited.

» *Transferability of skills.* While the teaching for professional practice principle aims to develop universal and transferable skills, the extent to which these skills can be transferred effectively to different legal contexts or other disciplines is uncertain. The principle therefore has potential relevance beyond the discipline of law, but challenges may arise in assessing and applying these skills in diverse professional settings.

CHAPTER 6

Building resilience and improving engagement for widening participation students

This theme focuses mainly on the students and on the challenges that law teachers felt students faced, as well as the problems tutors encountered in relation to students. It emerged out of the data in part as a result of identifying thematic links between the 'student engagement' and 'widening participation' codes. Key to this theme was the idea of building resilience for widening participation students, particularly through collaboration.

While much of the evidence from participants here (e.g. within the sub-codes of motivation and confidence) tended to focus on issues concerning student engagement, which are reflected in the wider literature,[1] there was also a recognition that the fault often lay not with students but with external factors – not least factors connected with widening participation backgrounds. In her interview, for instance, Laura made several references to the particular features and backgrounds of the students whom she taught. For example, she described them as 'time-poor' and described their language skills as being a 'massive issue'. They had a wide range of additional needs 'that mean quite often they are required to have alternative assessments or special arrangements made', and, especially when it came to legal skills, there was a 'lot of front loading of core academic skills that have to be there even before you can begin to springboard into more practice-based work'.

Laura also felt that her students benefited from having assessment tasks tailored to them. Some were, in her view, 'more comfortable working in a space where they, you know, have a clear structure and a clear task', while others in her experience 'are really uncomfortable in the world of: there is no right answer, come up with your argument and then you know, elaborate and debate'. Indeed, a lot of the data in the interviews (e.g. within the sub-codes of emotional support and curriculum design) consisted of participants describing in detail how aware they were of the challenges facing students and the innovative measures they had developed to counter these issues, often making use of examples of authentic teaching and assessment in the process (e.g. classroom collaboration). For instance, Nora talked about limited resources as being one of the many challenges of teaching at a widening participation institution in comparison with a university that had students from more traditional backgrounds. She said that one of the ways in which she addressed this was by putting her students in groups to do problem questions, as she felt that 'they are much better collaborating together'.

As I said in the book's preface, student engagement is key to any employability-related curriculum reform, and contextualizing classroom experiences for students is one way of fostering this. In addressing the problem of student disengagement, it has been noted that engagement has clear links with a student's motivation to learn[2] and that emotions and their engagement are an important issue in focusing and retaining attention. Improving student engagement is therefore a first step in beginning to resolve some fairly crucial student skills shortages, including problem solving, research and confidence.

Student engagement has also been identified as intrinsic to authentic assessment.[3] In this context it is again worth highlighting the CARE framework, which is also based around the same sort of student-centric factors identified within this theme and relies on student engagement for the implementation of its combination of compassionate, attentive, reason-based and empathetic teaching of legal skills. Much of the focus here is on building resilience within students, particularly those from widening participation backgrounds, in order to encourage engagement, hence the designation chosen for this theme.

It was notable that innovation through authentic assessment seemed to be regarded by the participants in my research as one of the more effective ways of tackling the issue of student disengagement. This theme therefore suggests a potential principle to add to an authentic assessment framework for legal education in relation to teaching to build resilience and improve engagement. However, there may be limited resources for making the required changes to assessment, and the work can be 'very intensive for the module leader, being extremely hands-on in terms of availability to students'.[4] How this pressure on resources and staff is handled and what could be done to alleviate it in the future seems worthy of further consideration, given the possible benefits to resilience and engagement for widening participation students in terms of working collaboratively inside and outside the classroom, as identified under this theme.

THE TEACHING FOR RESILIENCE AND ENGAGEMENT PRINCIPLE

The teaching for resilience and engagement principle developed out of the theme of building resilience and improving engagement for widening participation students and the codes on 'student engagement' and 'widening participation'.

The resilience principle focuses on the idea of building resilience for widening participation students through aspects of authentic assessment, such as collaboration, in particular, in order to address issues of student engagement. In relation to the widening participation code, the importance both of appropriate curriculum design and of emotional support for students was accentuated by the division of this code into named sub-codes based on these two issues.

Attentive teaching is the aspect of the CARE framework that aligns most closely with the resilience principle, based as it is on encouraging student participation. However, the teaching for resilience and engagement principle goes further than attentive teaching by placing an emphasis on students from widening participation backgrounds (unsurprisingly, given the context for this study) and applying relevant facets of academic opinion on authentic assessment. It has been suggested, for instance, that authentic assessment should stimulate students to engage in solving problems, applying their knowledge and making decisions.[5] This has benefits beyond simply improving student participation and building their resilience, however, as this sort of engagement is also potentially conducive to the development of their cognitive and thinking skills.

In discussing resilience it must be recognized that there is no universally agreed definition of the term. I would, however, take the view that resilience is a complex characteristic, related to aspects of not only the individual but also the environment they are in. I also believe that an individual's resilience, or ability to cope, may vary between different settings.

This principle also suggests practical solutions, particularly in terms of classroom collaboration, to address the challenges of engaging students that are supported in the literature. For example, although this view can be contested, it has been suggested that small-group work can be used to protect against dropout and encourage student engagement.

An equally important factor arising out of this research, however, was that the resilience principle also seemed to encourage the use of interventions outside the classroom in order to address issues relating to engagement and participation. Several aspects of this were raised by study participants: more tailoring of assessments to students (this includes in relation to teaching, through use of formative assessment that was more tailored to summative assessment), getting students to engage more with reading core legal texts (by demonstrating their usefulness both to developing legal skills and to legal practice), and providing additional feedback and support for students outside the classroom (including how to deal with distress, anxiety and depression).

Like the teaching for professional practice principle, this principle potentially covers more than one element of the Statement. Most directly, the resilience principle exemplifies the requirement for SQE candidates to learn to manage themselves and their own work by demonstrating how to initiate, plan, prioritize and manage work activities efficiently, punctually and to an appropriate standard, including dealing effectively with unforeseen circumstances. But the teaching for resilience and engagement principle also reflects the Statement's requirement for working with other people, including where it refers to 'responding to and addressing individual characteristics effectively and sensitively', 'treating others with courtesy and respect' and 'being supportive of colleagues'.[6]

Working in an autonomous way is also one of the requirements for a legal practitioner to be considered professionally responsible. While law teachers listening to, supporting and generally 'being there' for their students is key to the resilience principle, it is perhaps equally crucial in relation to this aspect of the PREPS framework for those teachers to instil these qualities in their students, so that the students can learn how to work both autonomously and with others in an efficient and effective manner. This will only be possible through incorporating explicit module learning objectives in relation to engagement, participation and collaboration into the law curriculum.

HOW THE TEACHING FOR RESILIENCE AND ENGAGEMENT PRINCIPLE CAN WORK IN PRACTICE

The teaching for resilience and engagement principle can be implemented in various ways to effectively support students from widening participation backgrounds. Some practical strategies that can be employed are given below.

Curriculum design

Curriculum design plays a critical role in promoting inclusivity and ensuring that legal education is relevant, relatable and engaging for students from diverse backgrounds. By designing the curriculum with inclusivity in mind, educators can create a learning experience that respects and values the unique perspectives and experiences of all students. In designing an inclusive curriculum, it is important to consider the following aspects.

Relevance and context

Incorporate real-life examples, case studies and scenarios that reflect a variety of legal contexts and perspectives. By presenting legal issues in a relatable and meaningful way, students will better understand the practical applications of the law and its impact on different communities. This approach helps students connect theoretical concepts to real-world situations, fostering a deeper understanding of the subject matter.

Diverse perspectives

Integrate diverse perspectives and voices throughout the curriculum. This includes incorporating readings, case studies and legal materials that represent a range of cultural, social and historical backgrounds. By exposing students to a variety of perspectives, they can develop a broader understanding of the law and its implications for different communities. It also promotes critical thinking and encourages students to question assumptions and biases that may influence legal decision making.

Active learning and application

Design the curriculum to emphasize active learning and the application of knowledge. This can be achieved through practical exercises, problem-solving tasks, simulations and experiential learning opportunities. By engaging students in hands-on activities, they can develop practical skills, enhance their problem-solving abilities and gain confidence in their ability to apply legal knowledge to real-world scenarios. This approach encourages active participation and fosters a deeper understanding of the subject matter.

Flexibility and adaptability

Design the curriculum in a way that allows for flexibility and adaptability to meet the diverse needs and interests of students. Provide opportunities for students to explore specialized areas of law or to pursue topics of personal interest. This flexibility allows students to tailor their learning experience, encourages their autonomy and supports their professional development based on their unique career aspirations.

Assessment and feedback

Align assessment methods with the curriculum's goals and ensure they are inclusive and equitable. Provide a variety of assessment formats that accommodate different learning styles and preferences. Additionally, provide timely and constructive feedback that helps students understand both their strengths and their areas for improvement. This feedback supports students' professional growth and development and fosters a culture of continuous learning.

Collaboration and dialogue

Promote collaboration and dialogue among students to encourage the exchange of ideas, perspectives and experiences. Incorporate group projects, discussions and interactive activities that foster teamwork and cooperation. This approach not only enhances learning through shared knowledge but also cultivates an inclusive and supportive classroom environment in which diverse voices are valued and respected.

Ongoing evaluation and improvement

Continuously evaluate and reflect on the effectiveness of the curriculum design. Seek feedback from students, faculty and professionals in the legal field to identify areas for improvement and make necessary adjustments. This iterative process ensures that the curriculum remains responsive to the evolving needs of students and the legal profession.

*

By designing the curriculum with inclusivity in mind, educators can create a learning environment that respects and celebrates diversity, promotes active engagement and prepares students to navigate the complexities of the legal profession. An inclusive curriculum design fosters a sense of belonging, empowers students to contribute their unique perspectives and equips them with the knowledge and skills necessary for a successful legal career in an increasingly diverse and interconnected world.

Authentic assessments

Authentic assessments play a crucial role in legal education by bridging the gap between theory and practice, and by preparing students for the challenges they will face in the real world of law. These assessments go beyond traditional examinations and tests, requiring students to apply their knowledge and skills to realistic legal scenarios, encouraging critical thinking, problem solving and decision making. Legal educators can consider the following approaches to implement authentic assessments.

Real-world scenarios

Design assessments that present students with authentic legal scenarios that they are likely to encounter in their professional careers. These scenarios can involve complex legal issues, client problems or ethical dilemmas. By presenting these real-world scenarios, students are challenged to analyse the facts, identify relevant legal principles and propose appropriate solutions.

Practical tasks

Incorporate practical tasks that require students to demonstrate their legal skills in action. These tasks can include legal research assignments, case analysis, drafting legal documents or preparing oral arguments. By engaging in these practical tasks, students can gain hands-on experience and develop the skills needed to navigate legal practice.

Problem-solving exercises

Develop problem-solving exercises that simulate the challenges lawyers face when working with clients or in legal disputes. These exercises can involve negotiation simulations, mediation sessions or mock trials. Students are required to analyse the interests and objectives of different parties, identify potential solutions and effectively communicate and advocate for their clients' positions.

Team-based projects

Foster collaboration and teamwork by assigning group projects that require students to work together to solve complex legal problems. This can involve researching and analysing a legal issue, preparing a legal strategy or developing a comprehensive case plan. By working in teams, students can develop important interpersonal skills such as communication, negotiation and conflict resolution, which are essential in the legal profession.

Reflective assessments

Incorporate assessments that encourage students to reflect on their learning and professional development. This can involve self-assessment exercises, reflective journals or portfolio assessments. By reflecting on their experiences, students can gain insights into their strengths, weaknesses and areas for improvement, fostering a deeper understanding of their own professional growth.

Feedback and evaluation

Provide timely and constructive feedback to students on their performance in authentic assessments. This feedback should highlight areas of strength and provide guidance on areas for improvement. Additionally, consider incorporating peer assessment and self-assessment, allowing students to provide feedback to their peers and to reflect on their own progress. This feedback and evaluation process supports students' development and helps them build resilience in their legal practice.

Continuous improvement

Regularly evaluate and refine the authentic assessments based on feedback from students and stakeholders. Assessments should evolve to reflect changes in legal practice and align with the desired learning outcomes. This continuous improvement process ensures that assessments remain relevant, challenging and effective in preparing students for their professional careers.

*

By implementing authentic assessments, legal educators create opportunities for students to develop their critical-thinking skills, their problem-solving abilities and their decision-making capabilities in a practical context. These assessments foster student engagement, enhance the understanding of legal concepts, and build resilience and adaptability to real-world legal scenarios. Authentic assessments play a pivotal role in preparing students to become competent and effective legal professionals, capable of meeting the complex challenges of the legal profession.

Collaboration and group work

Incorporating collaboration and group work into legal education is a valuable strategy to enhance student learning and promote the essential skills needed in the legal profession. By engaging students in collaborative activities and group projects, educators create opportunities for peer interaction, teamwork and the development of communication and collaboration skills. Listed below are some ways to expand on the incorporation of collaboration and group work into legal education.

Group projects

Assign group projects that require students to work together to solve legal problems or complete complex tasks. These projects can involve legal research, case analysis or the development of legal strategies. By working collaboratively, students can pool their knowledge and perspectives, exchange ideas and learn from one another. This collaborative environment encourages active engagement and critical thinking and develops problem-solving skills.

Case studies

Use case studies that require students to analyse legal issues and discuss possible solutions in small groups. Case studies can provide a rich context for students to apply legal principles and develop their analytical skills. Working in groups allows students to engage in thoughtful discussions, debate different viewpoints and collectively arrive at well-reasoned conclusions.

Role-play exercises

Incorporate role-playing exercises that involve simulated legal scenarios and require students to work together to enact different roles and engage in legal simulations. This can include client interviews, negotiations or mock trials. By participating in these activities, students can develop their communication, negotiation and advocacy skills, as well as their ability to work collaboratively under realistic circumstances.

Peer learning

Foster peer-learning opportunities by encouraging students to engage in peer teaching and peer feedback. This can involve students presenting their work to their peers, conducting peer reviews of written assignments or organizing book groups. Peer learning allows students to benefit from diverse perspectives, deepen their understanding of legal concepts and develop their communication and leadership skills.

Problem-solving discussions

Facilitate group discussions that focus on solving legal problems or analysing complex legal issues. Encourage students to engage in critical thinking, share their insights and engage in respectful debates. These discussions can promote active learning, enhance students' analytical skills and encourage collaboration and teamwork.

Group presentations

Assign group presentations where students collaborate to research and present legal topics or cases. This activity requires students to divide tasks, coordinate their efforts and deliver a cohesive and informative presentation. Group presentations can develop students' research, presentation and teamwork skills while fostering a supportive environment for constructive feedback and peer learning.

Online collaboration tools

Use online collaboration tools and platforms that facilitate group work and enhance communication among students. These tools can allow students to collaborate on projects, share documents and communicate asynchronously. Online platforms can also enable students to engage in virtual teamwork, overcoming geographical limitations and promoting inclusivity in collaborative activities.

*

By incorporating collaborative activities and group projects, legal educators can provide students with valuable opportunities to develop their teamwork, communication and collaboration skills. These experiences mirror the collaborative nature of legal practice, where lawyers often work in teams to address complex legal issues.

Moreover, by engaging in collaborative learning, students can benefit from the diverse perspectives and insights of their peers, they can broaden their understanding of legal concepts, and they can acquire the interpersonal skills necessary for effective teamwork in the legal profession.

Emotional support and mentorship

In addition to providing academic instruction, it is essential for legal education institutions to offer emotional support and mentorship programmes to students, particularly those from widening participation backgrounds. Recognizing and addressing the emotional wellbeing of students is crucial for their overall success and personal growth. Some ways to expand on the implementation of emotional support and mentorship programmes in legal education are given below.

One-on-one discussions

Establish a system in which students can have regular one-on-one discussions with faculty members, advisors or mentors. These meetings can provide a safe space for students to share their concerns, seek guidance and receive personalized support. Faculty members and mentors can offer empathetic listening, validate students' experiences, and provide advice and resources to help students navigate challenges.

Counselling services

Make counselling services available to students, either through on-campus professionals or by partnering with external organizations. Trained counsellors can offer confidential support to students who may be experiencing stress, anxiety or other emotional difficulties. These services can help students develop coping mechanisms, manage their mental health and build resilience.

Peer mentorship programmes

Implement peer mentorship programmes where upper-year students or alumni mentor incoming students. Peer mentors can offer guidance, share their experiences and provide emotional support to help new students navigate the transition to law school. This peer-to-peer connection can foster a sense of belonging, alleviate feelings of isolation and provide a valuable support network.

Workshops and training

Conduct workshops and training sessions that focus on emotional wellbeing, stress management and the building of resilience. These sessions can provide students with practical tools and strategies to cope with the demands of legal education. Topics may include time management, self-care, mindfulness and effective communication skills.

Widening participation initiatives

Develop targeted initiatives and programmes aimed specifically at supporting students from widening participation backgrounds. These programmes can include mentorship opportunities, networking events and resources tailored to their unique needs and challenges. By addressing the specific barriers these students may face, institutions can promote inclusivity and ensure equitable access to emotional support.

Community building

Foster a sense of community and belonging within the student body by organizing social events and by providing clubs and organizations that encourage peer connections and support networks. Creating spaces for students to interact, collaborate and build relationships with their peers can enhance their emotional wellbeing and create a supportive environment.

Holistic approach

Adopt a holistic approach to legal education that acknowledges the interconnectedness of academic, professional and personal development. Recognize that students' emotional wellbeing can impact on their academic performance and professional growth. By integrating emotional support initiatives into the curriculum and overall educational experience, institutions can nurture students' holistic development and equip them with the tools they need to thrive in the legal profession.

*

Emotional support and mentorship programmes play a crucial role in fostering a supportive and inclusive learning environment in which students feel valued, understood and empowered. By addressing the emotional needs of students, institutions can enhance their overall wellbeing, can promote resilience, and, ultimately, can contribute to their success in legal education and in future legal careers.

Tailored feedback and support

In legal education, providing tailored feedback and support is essential to guide students' progress, enhance their learning outcomes and promote continuous improvement. Below are some ways to expand on the implementation of tailored feedback and support in legal education.

Timely and constructive feedback

Ensure that students receive timely and constructive feedback on their work. This feedback should be specific and clear, and it should be focused on both strengths and areas for improvement. Faculty members can provide written comments, hold feedback sessions or schedule individual meetings to discuss assignments, examinations or other assessments. Timely feedback enables students to reflect on their performance, understand their strengths and weaknesses, and make necessary adjustments for future assignments.

Individualized support

Recognize that students may have different learning styles, abilities and areas of difficulty. Offer individualized support to address each student's specific needs. This can involve providing additional resources, such as supplementary materials, book guides or online tutorials, to help students grasp challenging concepts or improve their skills. Individualized support can also include arranging one-on-one sessions with faculty members or teaching assistants to provide personalized guidance and assistance.

Targeted workshops and tutorials

Organize workshops and tutorials that focus on addressing common areas of difficulty or specific skill development. These sessions can provide targeted instruction, practice opportunities and strategies for improvement. Workshops can cover topics such as legal research techniques, writing effective legal arguments, oral presentation skills or exam preparation. By targeting specific areas of concern, students can receive tailored support to enhance their performance in those areas.

Peer review and collaboration

Incorporate peer review activities in which students provide feedback on their classmates' work. Peer feedback not only lightens the workload for faculty members but also encourages students to actively engage with the work of their peers, to develop critical-thinking skills and to gain insights from different perspectives. Structured peer review processes can help students learn from one another, identify areas for improvement and refine their own work through constructive critique.

Academic support centres

Establish academic support centres or writing centres that provide additional resources and assistance to students. These centres can offer writing consultations, book skill workshops and subject-specific tutoring. Trained tutors or teaching assistants can provide guidance on writing strategies, time management, exam preparation and understanding course material. Academic support centres can serve as valuable resources for students seeking extra help or guidance outside of the classroom.

Progress tracking and goal setting

Implement mechanisms to track students' progress and help them set goals for their learning and development. This can involve regular check-ins, self-assessment exercises or individual learning plans. By setting goals and monitoring progress, students can take ownership of their learning journey, identify areas that require additional attention and actively work towards achieving their academic and professional objectives.

Continuous support

Ensure that support and feedback are provided throughout the academic year, not just during key assessments. Encourage students to seek assistance whenever needed, whether it is for clarifying concepts, discussing concerns or obtaining guidance. Establish an 'open door' policy where students feel comfortable approaching faculty members, teaching assistants or academic advisers for support. Regular communication and ongoing support can contribute to a positive learning experience and foster a sense of community and collaboration.

*

By providing tailored feedback and support, institutions can help students overcome challenges, refine their skills and reach their full potential. The combination of timely and constructive feedback, individualized support, targeted workshops, peer collaboration and access to academic support centres creates a comprehensive support system that empowers students to excel in their legal education and future legal careers.

Engaging teaching methods

To create an engaging learning environment in legal education, it is crucial to use interactive and innovative teaching methods that foster student participation, critical thinking and active engagement. Some strategies for expanding on engaging teaching methods in legal education are given below.

Discussions and debates

Incorporate discussions and debates into the classroom to encourage students to explore diverse perspectives, analyse legal issues and develop their analytical and communication skills. Engage students in meaningful conversations that require them to evaluate different arguments, propose solutions and defend their positions. This interactive approach promotes critical thinking, active listening and the ability to articulate legal reasoning.

Simulations and role plays

Introduce simulations and role plays that allow students to immerse themselves in realistic legal scenarios. By assuming the roles of lawyers, judges or clients, students can apply legal principles actively, practise problem solving and develop their professional skills. Simulations can include mock trials, client interviews, negotiation exercises or drafting legal documents. These activities can provide hands-on experience, enhance practical skills and build students' confidence in their professional interactions.

Case studies and real-life examples

Use case studies and real-life examples to connect legal theory with practical applications. Presenting students with authentic cases or scenarios helps them understand the real-world implications of legal concepts, develop problem-solving abilities and analyse legal issues in context. Case studies can encourage students to think critically, evaluate evidence and apply legal principles to resolve complex problems.

Technology integration

Incorporate technology tools and platforms to enhance student engagement and facilitate interactive learning experiences. Use online discussion forums, virtual simulations or collaborative platforms to promote active participation, knowledge sharing and group collaboration. Virtual reality or augmented reality can be used to create immersive experiences that simulate legal environments and enhance student learning.

Active learning techniques

Employ active learning techniques that involve students in the learning process. These can include small-group activities, brainstorming sessions, peer teaching or problem-based learning. By actively participating in their own learning, students can develop a deeper understanding of legal concepts, improve their critical-thinking skills and retain information more effectively. These methods can enhance student participation and active engagement with the subject matter.

Multimedia and visual aids

Use multimedia resources, visual aids and interactive presentations to enhance engagement and facilitate comprehension. Incorporate videos, audio recordings, infographics or interactive learning modules to illustrate complex legal concepts, present case studies or demonstrate legal procedures. Multimedia elements can capture students' attention, appeal to different learning styles and promote a more dynamic learning experience.

Field trips and guest speakers

Organize field trips to legal institutions, courtrooms or law firms, or invite guest speakers from the legal profession to share their experiences and insights. Exposing students to real-world legal environments and practitioners helps them connect theory to practice, understand the application of legal concepts and gain valuable industry perspectives. Guest speakers can provide first-hand knowledge, professional anecdotes and practical advice that enrich students' understanding of the legal profession.

*

By incorporating these engaging teaching methods, legal educators can create an interactive and stimulating learning environment that fosters student participation, critical thinking and active engagement with the subject matter. These strategies can promote a deeper understanding of legal concepts, enhance practical skills and prepare students for the challenges and complexities of the legal profession.

Community building

In legal education, fostering a sense of belonging and community within the classroom is essential for creating a supportive and inclusive learning environment. Some strategies for expanding on community building in legal education are listed below.

Icebreakers and team-building activities

Begin the course with icebreaker activities and team-building exercises to help students get to know each other and establish connections. These activities can include introductions, sharing personal experiences or interests, or collaborative problem-solving tasks. By creating a positive and inclusive atmosphere from the start, students are more likely to feel comfortable engaging with their peers and contributing to class discussions.

Classroom norms and expectations

Establish classroom norms and expectations collaboratively with students. Encourage open dialogue about mutual respect, active listening and valuing diverse perspectives. Setting ground rules collectively helps create a safe and inclusive space in which everyone feels respected and heard. It also promotes a sense of ownership and shared responsibility within the classroom community.

Group work and collaboration

Incorporate group work and collaborative projects into the curriculum to encourage students to work together towards common goals. Assigning diverse groups and rotating group members throughout the semester allows students to interact with classmates from different backgrounds and perspectives. This collaboration can foster teamwork, promote understanding of different viewpoints and enhance communication and interpersonal skills.

Peer learning and mentoring

Encourage peer learning and mentoring by pairing students with different levels of experience or expertise. Establish a buddy system where more experienced students can support and guide their peers. Peer mentoring not only promotes a sense of community but also facilitates knowledge sharing, skills development and the building of professional relationships.

Active listening and respectful communication

Emphasize the importance of active listening and respectful communication in the classroom. Encourage students to engage in active listening by giving their full attention to their peers, asking clarifying questions and providing constructive feedback. Foster an environment in which diverse viewpoints are valued and respected, and teach students effective communication techniques to facilitate productive discussions and debates.

Inclusive language and representation

Use inclusive language and diverse examples in teaching materials and discussions. Ensure that the curriculum represents a wide range of perspectives, experiences and identities. This fosters inclusivity, recognizes students' diverse backgrounds and promotes a sense of belonging for all students.

Celebrate achievements and successes

Recognize and celebrate students' achievements and successes in their academic and professional endeavours. Highlight individual and group accomplishments, such as excellent performance in assignments, successful moot court competitions or internships. Publicly acknowledging students' efforts and achievements reinforces a positive and supportive classroom environment.

Collaborative classroom activities

Foster a sense of belonging and community within the classroom. Incorporate collaborative classroom activities that promote teamwork, problem solving and critical thinking. These can include group discussions, case analysis, mock trials or negotiation exercises. Encourage students to share their perspectives, insights and experiences, and facilitate discussions in which everyone's input is valued and respected, creating a supportive and inclusive learning environment.

Office hours and individual support

Provide regular office hours or individual support sessions where students can seek guidance, ask questions or discuss concerns. Offering one-on-one support and mentorship helps students feel valued, supported and connected to their tutors. It also provides an opportunity for personalized feedback and advice tailored to their individual needs.

*

By implementing these community-building strategies, educators can create a classroom environment that promotes a sense of belonging, inclusivity and collaboration. This fosters student engagement, active participation and a supportive learning community where students feel comfortable sharing their experiences, perspectives and insights.

Continuous reflection and improvement

Continuous reflection and improvement are crucial aspects of creating an effective and inclusive learning environment. Below are some ways to expand on the concept of continuous reflection and improvement in legal education.

Student feedback surveys

Conduct regular surveys or feedback sessions to gather input from students about their learning experiences. Ask specific questions about the implemented strategies, the classroom environment and the support initiatives. Encourage students to provide constructive feedback and suggestions for improvement. Analyse the feedback received and identify areas where adjustments can be made to better meet students' needs and enhance their learning experience.

Reflective teaching practice

Engage in personal reflection as an educator to evaluate the effectiveness of the implemented strategies. Reflect on the strengths and weaknesses of different teaching approaches, activities and support initiatives. Consider how these elements can contribute to student engagement, learning outcomes and the overall classroom environment. Use self-reflection to identify areas for improvement and develop an action plan for implementing changes.

Collaborative professional development

Participate in professional development opportunities focused on inclusive teaching practices and effective student support. Engage with colleagues; attend workshops, conferences or webinars; and share experiences and best practices. Collaborative professional development allows for knowledge sharing, exposure to innovative teaching methods and the exchange of ideas for continuous improvement.

Data analysis and assessment

Analyse student performance data, assessment outcomes and learning analytics to identify patterns and trends. Look for areas where students may be struggling or excelling, and determine if adjustments to teaching methods or support initiatives are needed. Use data-informed decision making to tailor instruction and interventions to better meet student needs and promote academic success.

Pedagogical research and innovation

Stay informed about current research and innovations in legal education pedagogy. Explore scholarly articles, journals and books that discuss effective teaching strategies and techniques. Consider adopting new approaches, technologies or instructional methods that can align with research findings and support student learning and engagement. Embrace a growth mindset that embraces experimentation and embraces innovation to continually improve the learning experience.

Faculty collaboration and peer feedback

Foster a culture of collaboration among faculty members. Encourage peer observation and feedback where tutors observe each other's classes and provide constructive input. This process allows for the exchange of ideas, the sharing of effective teaching practices and the identification of areas for improvement. Peer feedback provides valuable insights and encourages legal educators to reflect on their teaching methods and make necessary adjustments.

Ongoing communication with students

Maintain open lines of communication with students throughout the semester. Encourage them to share their thoughts, concerns and suggestions on an ongoing basis. Provide opportunities for students to provide anonymous feedback or engage in class discussions about their learning experiences. Regular communication allows legal educators to address student needs promptly and make adjustments as necessary.

*

By incorporating continuous reflection and improvement into legal education, instructors can create a dynamic and responsive learning environment. This approach ensures that teaching methods, support initiatives and classroom practices are regularly assessed, refined and adapted to meet the evolving needs of students. By seeking feedback, analysing data, staying informed about current research and collaborating with peers, legal educators can create an engaging and inclusive learning experience that fosters student success.

Collaboration with support services

Collaborating with support services within the institution is essential for providing a comprehensive and holistic approach to student support. Some ways of expanding on the concept of collaboration with support services in legal education are given below.

Academic advisers

Work closely with academic advisers who can provide guidance and support to students regarding course selection, degree requirements and academic planning. Collaborate with advisers to ensure that students receive accurate and up-to-date information about the legal curriculum, prerequisites and progression pathways. By maintaining regular communication with academic advisers, legal educators can help students make informed decisions about their academic journey and align their coursework with their career goals.

Career counsellors

Partner with career counsellors who specialize in the legal field to offer students guidance and resources for career development. Collaborate with career services to organize workshops, seminars or guest speaker events that are focused on legal career opportunities, job search strategies and professional networking. By working together, instructors and career counsellors can provide students with a comprehensive understanding of the legal profession and equip them with the necessary skills and resources to succeed in their career aspirations.

Student wellbeing teams

Collaborate with student wellbeing teams or counselling services to support students' mental health and wellbeing. Foster a proactive approach to student wellbeing by integrating discussions on stress management, self-care and work–life balance into the curriculum. Provide resources and referrals to support services for students who may be facing personal challenges or experiencing emotional difficulties. By working together with wellbeing teams, legal educators can contribute to creating a supportive and caring learning environment that promotes the overall wellbeing of students.

Accommodation services

Collaborate with accommodation services or disability support offices to ensure that students with disabilities or specific learning needs receive appropriate accommodations. Engage in discussions with accommodation specialists to understand the specific needs of individual students, and make necessary adjustments to teaching methods, assessments or classroom arrangements. By working in tandem with accommodation services, legal educators can ensure that all students have equal access to learning opportunities and can thrive in the legal education environment.

Cultural and diversity support

Collaborate with cultural and diversity support services to promote inclusivity and address the unique challenges faced by students from diverse backgrounds. Seek guidance and resources to create an inclusive learning environment that respects and celebrates diversity. Incorporate culturally responsive teaching practices that recognize and value students' different experiences and perspectives. By collaborating with cultural and diversity support services, legal educators can contribute to a more inclusive legal education environment in which all students feel valued and empowered.

Student support referrals

Familiarize yourself with the various support services available on campus, and provide students with appropriate referrals when needed. Maintain an updated list of resources and contacts for academic, career, wellbeing and other support services that students can access. By actively connecting students with the appropriate support services, legal educators can help students navigate challenges and ensure they receive the necessary support to thrive academically and personally.

Professional development

Engage in professional development opportunities that enhance your knowledge and skills in collaborating with support services. Attend workshops, seminars and training sessions focused on effective collaboration and communication with support staff. By expanding your understanding of the roles and expertise of different support services, you can effectively collaborate and leverage their resources to support student success.

*

Collaborating with support services within the institution enhances the overall resilience and engagement of students in legal education. By working together, legal educators and support services can provide comprehensive support that addresses students' academic, career and wellbeing needs. This collaborative approach creates a supportive ecosystem in which students receive the guidance, resources and assistance they need to thrive academically and personally.

Professional role models

Incorporating professional role models into legal education can have a profound impact on students' motivation, inspiration and career aspirations. Below are some ways to expand on the concept of connecting students with legal professionals.

Guest lectures

Organize guest lectures or panel discussions where legal professionals from diverse backgrounds can share their experiences, insights and career journeys with students. Invite professionals who have achieved success in distinct legal fields, such as private practice, public interest proceedings, corporate law and government legal services. These guest speakers can provide real-world perspectives on the challenges, rewards and opportunities within their respective areas of expertise. Hearing directly from professionals who have navigated similar paths can inspire students and provide valuable guidance as they explore their own legal careers.

Networking events

Arrange networking events where students can have the opportunity to interact with legal professionals. These events can take the form of career fairs, alumni networking receptions or industry-specific gatherings. Encourage students to actively engage with professionals, ask questions and seek advice on career development. By facilitating connections between students and professionals, networking events create a platform for meaningful interactions, mentorship opportunities and the establishment of valuable professional relationships.

Mentoring programmes

Implement mentoring programmes that pair students with legal professionals who serve as mentors. Mentoring relationships provide students with personalized guidance, support and encouragement. Match mentors and mentees based on shared interests, backgrounds or career goals. Mentors can offer insights into the legal profession, provide career advice, help navigate professional challenges and offer valuable feedback on students' professional development. Regular mentor–mentee meetings or events can foster a strong sense of support, guidance and camaraderie.

Alumni engagement

Leverage the alumni network of the institution to connect students with successful legal professionals who are alumni. Organize alumni networking events, career panels and mentorship programmes specifically tailored to alumni involvement. Alumni can offer unique insights into the legal profession, provide guidance on career paths and share their personal experiences transitioning from law school to practice. Engaging alumni as role models fosters a sense of community and continuity, allowing current students to benefit from the experiences and successes of those who have preceded them.

Professional development workshops

Arrange professional development workshops facilitated by legal professionals who can offer expertise in specific areas of law and legal practice. These workshops can focus on practical skills, emerging trends and specialized areas of law. Professionals can provide hands-on training, share case studies and offer practical insights into the day-to-day realities of legal practice. Not only can such workshops enhance students' knowledge and skills, they can also expose them to different professional roles and potential career paths.

Diversity and inclusion initiatives

Emphasize the importance of diverse role models by actively seeking legal professionals from underrepresented groups as guest speakers, mentors or panellists. Highlight their experiences and accomplishments to showcase the diversity within the legal profession and inspire students from all backgrounds. By promoting diversity and inclusion, legal education can challenge stereotypes, foster inclusivity and provide opportunities for students to connect with professionals who share similar backgrounds or identities.

*

Connecting students with legal professionals through guest lectures, networking events, mentoring programmes and other initiatives helps bridge the gap between academic learning and real-world legal practice. These interactions can expose students to diverse perspectives, inspire them to envision their own career paths, and provide practical guidance for their professional journeys. By showcasing successful legal professionals as role models, students are empowered to overcome challenges, set ambitious goals and pursue fulfilling careers in the legal field.

SUMMARY OF KEY MESSAGES

The teaching for resilience and engagement principle can work in practice

- by designing the curriculum with inclusivity in mind;
- by implementing authentic assessments that mirror real-world legal scenarios and require critical thinking, problem solving and decision making;
- by incorporating collaborative activities and group projects that encourage peer interaction and teamwork;

- by offering emotional support and mentorship programmes to students, particularly those from widening participation backgrounds;
- by providing timely and constructive feedback on students' work to guide their progress and improvement;
- by utilizing interactive and engaging teaching methods, such as discussions, debates, simulations and role plays;
- by fostering a sense of belonging and community within the classroom;
- by reflecting regularly on the effectiveness of the implemented strategies and seeking feedback from students;
- by collaborating with support services within one's home institution, such as academic advisers, career counsellors and student wellbeing teams; and
- by connecting students with legal professionals from diverse backgrounds through guest lectures, networking events and mentoring programmes.

By incorporating these strategies and tailoring them to the specific needs of students from widening participation backgrounds, the teaching for resilience and engagement principle can effectively support students in their academic and professional development. It creates an inclusive and empowering learning environment that nurtures resilience, enhances engagement and equips students with the necessary skills and attributes to succeed in the legal profession. However, the following challenges can be identified. Addressing these issues requires careful planning, collaboration and ongoing assessment and adaptation. Institutions and educators need to recognize the unique contexts and needs of their students and be prepared to invest time, resources and effort into creating an environment that fosters student engagement and resilience.

HINTS AND TIPS

» *Implementation in diverse contexts.* The teaching for resilience and engagement principle, as presented, may face challenges when applied in different educational contexts, with some institutional

settings, cultural backgrounds and student populations presenting difficulties. What works effectively in one context may not necessarily work as well in another, and this requires careful consideration and adaptation.
» *Resistance from traditional teaching practices.* Introducing a new principle that emphasizes resilience and engagement may face resistance from teachers who are accustomed to more traditional teaching methods. Encouraging a shift in pedagogical approaches and mindset can be challenging, as it requires buy-in and support from faculty members and administrators.
» *Faculty training and development.* Implementing the teaching for resilience and engagement principle is likely to require training and professional development for faculty members in order to equip them with the necessary knowledge and skills to effectively support student engagement and resilience. However, providing comprehensive and ongoing training opportunities for faculty can be resource intensive and time consuming.
» *Assessment and evaluation.* Designing and implementing authentic assessments that promote engagement and resilience can be complex. Developing appropriate assessment criteria, providing meaningful feedback and ensuring fairness and validity can be challenging. Additionally, evaluating the effectiveness of these assessments in measuring student engagement and resilience presents its own set of challenges.
» *Resource limitations.* Implementing strategies to promote student engagement and resilience may require additional resources, including technology, collaborative spaces and support services. Institutions with limited resources may face difficulties in providing the necessary infrastructure and support to fully implement the teaching for resilience and engagement principle.
» *Student diversity and individual needs.* Students come from diverse backgrounds with varying learning styles, motivations and support needs. Adapting teaching approaches to meet the individual needs of students and promote their engagement and resilience can be a complex and demanding task for educators.
» *Sustainability and scalability.* Ensuring the long-term sustainability and scalability of initiatives that promote student

engagement and resilience can be challenging. Institutions need to consider how to embed these principles into the broader curriculum and educational practices and how to ensure ongoing support and evaluation.

CHAPTER 7

Teacher and student adaptation to changing environments

This theme, which is related mainly to external factors that impact on education, emerged from the data and arose in part from the thematic links between the 'technology' and 'pandemic' codes. Many of the challenges and opportunities of adapting to new teaching technologies that participants spoke about were prompted by the institutional response to the pandemic (although the pandemic response went beyond simply technological factors). More specifically, this theme came out of the data that helped to identify how law teachers responded to challenges presented by external factors that forced them to change or adapt their teaching, and it highlighted instances where this was used as an opportunity to introduce or refine authentic learning and assessment.

There was some overlap in the data between participants talking about the impact of technology (particularly remote learning) on legal skills teaching and the effect of the coronavirus pandemic. Justin, for example, talked about finding it hard to get students to 'turn on the camera, and there were very big pauses and very big silence' when he first started teaching online as a result of the pandemic.

The use of technology in legal skills teaching, often introduced in response to Covid-19 lockdown restrictions, presented challenges to the law teachers in my study, mainly in terms of getting used to new teaching platforms such as Teams. However, these challenges and the response to them inadvertently allowed legal education to reflect legal practice more closely in some respects. In particular, there was a greater use of technology than might otherwise have been the case had there not been an external driver that was as disruptive as the pandemic. This shift involved law teachers adapting in ways that they were not traditionally used to doing, particularly when it came to online learning.

The environment theme fits into the theoretical framework for this research by highlighting experiential learning as an element of authentic assessment. In experiential learning, learners learn through direct participation rather than through less active conventional teaching approaches. Kolb's learning cycle,[1] with its focus on students conceptualizing abstract principles and active experimentation, has been used to explore the potential of authentic learning activities as tools for experiential learning. Experiential learning also allows legal curricula to meet the goal of experiencing practice, as it can be a unique and constructive means of uniting formal knowledge and experience of practice.[2]

Studies have used technology – in the form of video game simulations[3] and field trips[4] – to encourage a wider, more contextualized consideration of legal concepts and values. Budgets and time constraints could be potential barriers to the utilisation of technology in the classroom, but the benefits – including contextualizing legal theory and helping students to focus on career options and possibilities – seem to be worth overcoming these challenges for. The evidence within this theme seems to offer the potential for legal skills teaching to reflect legal practice more authentically through technology in response to external factors, some of which were new and unexpected like the pandemic.

Using Justin as an example again, as well as referring to the challenges of teaching online, he also spoke about how he had overcome those challenges by adapting to this new environment. It is notable that Justin felt that engaging the students in this manner not only helped the online session flow more smoothly but also potentially helped to better prepare them for professional life. The environment theme therefore also highlights a key element of graduate attributes mentioned in chapter 1: the need for graduates to demonstrate flexibility and adaptability beyond their discipline-specific knowledge. In this sense, in terms of implications for improving authentic teaching and assessment practices, this theme seems to suggest the potential value of a principle based around teaching that adapts to the environment, which can be incorporated into a framework for authentic assessment and PBL in legal education. This principle will be explored further below.

TEACHING THAT ADAPTS TO THE ENVIRONMENT PRINCIPLE

Arising from the teacher and student adaptation to changing environments theme, the principle of teaching that adapts to the environment fits into the framework for authentic assessment in legal education developed for this study by highlighting experiential learning as a key element. This principle draws on data relating to the codes based on 'technology' and 'pandemic' to offer the potential for legal skills teaching to more authentically reflect legal practice through technology in response to external factors.

This principle represents a new element that is not part of the CARE framework at all, since it is based very much on the context in which this book was carried out: that is, a global pandemic that necessitated a shift to online teaching across the entire higher education sector. The direct effects of the pandemic in particular were captured by data linked to the sub-codes relating to rapid change, which concerned the disruptive impact of the health crisis, and future predictions, which is perhaps of more direct relevance here when it comes to potential interventions that can form part of the PREPS framework for authentic teaching and assessment in a legal context.

Key to the teaching that adapts to the environment principle is the effect of forcing both law teachers and students to engage with rapid change (in this case at a societal level as a result of the pandemic) by getting to grips with new platforms for learning and practice (i.e. online learning environments that simulate the real world of legal practice). Far from being a negative aspect, this can therefore be presented as a positive development, since it encourages a wider, more contextualized consideration of legal concepts and values for law students in a way that both directly reflects developments in the profession and benefits their future readiness for work. As stated in the preface, the pandemic has resulted in higher expectations among employers (such as law firms) when it comes to graduate employability skills, including in respect of information and communication technology skills.

The link with experiential learning also directly ties this theme into the literature on authentic assessment. Experiential learning is anchored in real-life experiences, and it has indeed been described as a form of both authentic assessment and PBL because of this potential to integrate students' experiences into the curriculum and allow them to view problems from a variety of different perspectives.

Budgets and time constraints have often been cited as restrictions on the use of experiential learning, but it may be that utilisation of online learning environments offers a way of getting around this expense. The level of investment in online teaching can vary, and, based on the experience of participants in my research, solutions can range from doing fairly basic online research tasks, to getting students to talk to each other more in online groups, or, at the highest level, using advanced software such as 'Practical Law' to create complex online simulations.[5]

Like the resilience principle, the environment principle crosses over the requirements under the Statement for SQE candidates to learn to manage themselves and their own work and to work with other people. Under these requirements, the Statement refers to aspects of the teaching that adapts to the environment principle as well as to data within the 'technology' and 'pandemic' codes, especially under the latter's sub-codes of rapid change and future predictions. This principle includes elements that come within the communication heading that cover 'using the most appropriate method and style of communication for the situation and the recipient',[6] which could include use of online communications where appropriate and necessary. Also, under the management heading, this would cover dealing with unforeseen circumstances and managing available resources efficiently, which would seem to include meeting external challenges such as the pandemic. A key element of graduate attributes is the need for graduates to demonstrate flexibility and adaptability beyond their discipline-specific knowledge, and this is highlighted by the environment principle. This also reflects another requirement of the Statement in relation to professionalism and judgment, where adapting legal practice to address developments is mentioned specifically as a desirable ability for candidates to demonstrate.

HOW THE PRINCIPLE OF TEACHING THAT ADAPTS TO THE ENVIRONMENT CAN WORK IN PRACTICE

Implementing the teaching that adapts to the environment principle in practice involves incorporating strategies and approaches that enable educators to adjust legal education to changing circumstances, particularly through the use of technology. Some practical considerations for integrating this principle are given below.

Technology integration

Integrating technology into legal education can enhance the learning experience and prepare students for the digital landscape of modern legal practice. Some ways of expanding on the concept of technology integration are listed below.

Online platforms and virtual classrooms

Implement online platforms and virtual classrooms that facilitate interactive and collaborative learning experiences. These platforms can host live lectures, discussions and group activities, allowing students to participate remotely and engage with course content in real time. Virtual classrooms also provide opportunities for breakout sessions, document sharing and collaborative problem solving. By leveraging online platforms, students can access course materials, submit assignments and engage with peers and faculty from anywhere, fostering flexibility and accessibility.

Digital tools for engagement

Use a variety of digital tools to promote engagement and interactivity. Online polling and quiz platforms can be used to assess students' understanding and promote active participation. Discussion forums and chat features can enable ongoing communication and encourage students to share their perspectives and engage in meaningful dialogue. Video-based platforms can enhance the delivery of instructional content, allowing faculty to incorporate multimedia elements, demonstrations and simulations. By leveraging digital tools, legal education can become more dynamic, interactive and learner centred.

Learning management systems (LMSs)

Implement a robust LMS that serves as a central hub for course materials, announcements, assignments and resources. An LMS provides a structured and organized framework for delivering content and tracking student progress. It can also facilitate communication between students and faculty, allowing for timely feedback and support. Additionally, an LMS can host online assessments, provide analytics on student performance, and support the integration of external legal research databases or resources.

Training and support

Provide comprehensive training and ongoing support for both educators and students to ensure effective utilization of technology. Offer workshops, tutorials or online resources that demonstrate how to use specific tools or platforms effectively. Legal educators can benefit from professional development opportunities focused on technology integration strategies and best practices. Students, on the other hand, may require orientation sessions or access to self-paced tutorials to familiarize themselves with the technology being used. Technical support should also be readily available to address any technical issues or challenges that may arise.

Access to legal research databases

Integrate access to legal research databases and resources within the digital learning environment. Provide students with guidance on using online legal research tools effectively and efficiently. By incorporating access to these resources, students can develop their research skills, explore real-world legal cases and precedents, and learn how to navigate the vast amount of legal information available online. This integration enhances students' ability to engage in legal analysis, critical thinking and evidence-based decision making.

Ethical and technological competence

Integrate discussions and assignments that address ethical considerations and professional responsibility in the digital age. By emphasizing the importance of maintaining client confidentiality, data security and ethical behaviour in the use of technology, legal educators can help students to develop a strong understanding of the ethical implications of technology in legal practice, including issues related to privacy, data protection and cyber security.

*

By embracing technology integration in legal education, institutions can create a more engaging, flexible and accessible learning environment. Students can develop digital literacy skills, collaborate effectively in virtual settings and gain practical experience with tools and platforms commonly used in legal practice. Moreover, technology integration prepares students to navigate the evolving technological landscape of the legal profession, enabling them to embrace innovation and adapt to emerging trends in the field.

Experiential learning opportunities

Experiential learning is a vital component of legal education as it enables students to bridge the gap between theory and practice. Expanding on the concept of experiential learning opportunities in legal education, some key points to consider are given below.

Case studies

Incorporate case studies that reflect real-world legal issues and dilemmas. These case studies can be drawn from actual legal cases or constructed to simulate realistic scenarios. By analysing and applying legal concepts to these cases, students develop critical-thinking and problem-solving skills. Case studies also provide opportunities for students to explore legal research, analysis and reasoning, preparing them for the complexities of legal practice.

Simulations and role playing

Use simulations and role-playing activities to immerse students in authentic legal scenarios. These activities can involve mock trials, client interviews, negotiation exercises or the drafting of legal documents. Simulations allow students to practise legal skills and experience the dynamics and challenges of legal practice in a controlled environment. Through role playing, students can develop effective communication, advocacy and negotiation skills, enhancing their professional competence and confidence.

Virtual internships

Leverage technology to offer virtual internships that provide students with hands-on experience working in legal settings. Virtual internships allow students to collaborate with practising lawyers, participate in legal research projects, assist with client matters and observe legal proceedings remotely. These experiences can help students to develop practical skills, gain exposure to the intricacies of legal practice and build professional networks.

Immersive simulations and virtual law firm environments

Use technology to create immersive simulations and virtual law firm environments. These digital platforms can replicate the day-to-day operations of a law firm, allowing students to engage in tasks such as conducting legal research, drafting documents and interacting with clients. Virtual law firm environments provide a safe and controlled space for students to apply legal concepts, work collaboratively and experience the challenges and dynamics of a legal practice. These simulations can be enhanced with interactive elements, feedback mechanisms and branching scenarios to provide a rich and engaging learning experience.

Technology-enhanced legal research

Design learning experiences that reflect real-world legal practice. Integrate technology into legal research activities to expose students to digital research tools, databases and resources commonly used in legal practice. Provide training and guidance on effectively using online legal research platforms, case law databases, legislative databases and legal research techniques. By incorporating technology-enhanced legal research, students can develop the skills necessary to navigate the vast amount of legal information that is available online, to evaluate the credibility and relevance of sources, and to apply their findings to legal problems.

Reflective practice

Incorporate opportunities for reflection and debriefing after experiential learning activities. Encourage students to analyse their experiences critically; identify strengths and areas for improvement; and reflect on the ethical, professional and practical implications of their actions. Facilitate discussions that promote self-reflection, peer feedback and faculty guidance to deepen students' understanding of the practicalities and complexities of legal practice.

*

By integrating experiential learning opportunities into legal education and leveraging technology to create realistic and immersive learning experiences, students can develop the skills, knowledge and professional attributes necessary for successful legal practice. These experiences foster critical-thinking, decision-making and problem-solving abilities, while also providing students with a glimpse into the realities of the legal profession.

Active learning approaches

Active learning approaches are highly effective in legal education as they promote student engagement, critical thinking and collaboration. Expanding on the concept of active learning, I now detail some key points to consider.

Online discussion boards

Use online discussion boards as a platform for student interaction and knowledge sharing. Assign discussion topics related to legal concepts, case studies or current legal issues, and encourage students to participate actively by sharing their perspectives, asking questions and engaging in respectful debates. Online discussions provide opportunities for students to express their thoughts, analyse legal arguments and develop their communication skills.

Group projects

Assign group projects that require students to work together to analyse complex legal problems or develop solutions to hypothetical scenarios. These projects can involve legal research, case analysis or the creation of legal documents. By collaborating with their peers, students learn to navigate diverse perspectives, negotiate different viewpoints and develop teamwork skills. Group projects can also foster a sense of shared responsibility and encourage students to rely on each other's strengths.

Virtual breakout rooms

Use virtual breakout rooms during online classes to facilitate small-group discussions and collaboration. Assign specific tasks or problems for students to solve together within these breakout rooms. Virtual breakout rooms allow for focused interactions, active participation and in-depth exploration of legal issues. Students can share ideas, challenge assumptions and arrive at well-reasoned conclusions collectively.

Problem-based learning

Incorporate PBL activities in which students are presented with real or hypothetical legal problems and are tasked with analysing the issues, identifying relevant legal principles and proposing solutions.

These activities can encourage students to think critically, apply their legal knowledge and develop problem-solving skills. PBL scenarios can be presented through case studies, hypothetical client situations or legal dilemmas, allowing students to engage with the complexities of legal practice.

Role play and mock scenarios

Introduce role playing and mock scenarios that simulate legal interactions and decision-making processes. For example, students can participate in simulated client interviews, negotiations or court proceedings. Role playing allows students to experience the practical aspects of legal practice; to develop professional skills such as active listening, effective communication and persuasive advocacy; and to gain a deeper understanding of the complexities of legal problem solving.

Formative assessments

Use formative assessments throughout the learning process to gauge student understanding and provide timely feedback. Formative assessments can take the form of quizzes, short assignments or in-class activities that allow students to apply their knowledge and receive feedback on their progress. These assessments promote active engagement with the material and help students identify areas for improvement.

*

By incorporating active learning approaches into legal education, students become active participants in their own learning process. They can develop critical-thinking, problem-solving and collaboration skills, preparing them for the demands of the legal profession. Active learning also fosters a deeper understanding of legal concepts and promotes lifelong learning by encouraging students to continuously engage with legal issues and develop their professional capabilities.

Flexibility and adaptability

Adaptability and flexibility are essential skills for success in legal practice. Expanding on the importance of these skills in legal education, some key points to consider are discussed below.

Unforeseen situations

Design activities and assignments that present students with unforeseen or complex legal situations. These scenarios can require students to analyse new legal developments, respond to changing regulations or navigate unexpected challenges. By engaging with these situations, students can learn to think critically, evaluate alternative approaches and make informed decisions under pressure.

Problem solving and critical thinking

Incorporate problem-solving activities that encourage students to think critically and find creative solutions to legal challenges. Presenting students with open-ended scenarios or ambiguous legal problems helps develop their ability to adapt and adjust their approach based on the unique circumstances of each case. This fosters their analytical skills, strategic thinking and ability to navigate complex legal issues.

Emerging technologies

Encourage students to explore and familiarize themselves with emerging technologies relevant to the legal field. Technology is transforming the legal landscape rapidly, and students need to be adaptable and open to leveraging new tools and platforms. Integrate assignments or discussions that require students to research and assess the implications of technology in legal practice, such as artificial intelligence, blockchain and online dispute resolution.

New legal developments

Emphasize the importance of staying updated on legal developments and trends. Provide opportunities for students to engage with current legal issues through case studies, discussions and research assignments. This cultivates their ability to adapt their legal strategies and arguments based on changing laws, court decisions and societal developments.

Professional skills training

Offer professional skills training, including exercises and simulations focused on adaptability and flexibility. For example, simulate challenging client interactions and unexpected courtroom situations in which students must adjust their approach and communicate effectively. These simulations can provide a safe space for students to practice adaptability skills, receive feedback and refine their professional abilities.

Reflective practice

Incorporate opportunities for students to reflect on their experiences and assess their adaptability skills. Encourage them to identify instances where they demonstrated flexibility, as well as areas where they could improve. Reflective practice helps students develop self-awareness, recognize their strengths and limitations, and cultivate a growth mindset.

*

By emphasizing adaptability and flexibility in legal education, students can develop the ability to navigate the ever-changing legal landscape. They can become adept at adjusting their strategies, thinking creatively and leveraging new technologies to address legal challenges effectively. These skills can prepare students for the dynamic nature of legal practice, enabling them to thrive in their careers and contribute to the evolving legal profession.

Authentic assessment

To align assessments with the principles of authentic assessment in legal education effectively, legal educators should consider the following points.

Real-world legal tasks

Design assessments that mirror the tasks and challenges encountered in real-world legal practice. This can include drafting legal documents, conducting legal research, analysing case studies and presenting oral arguments. By simulating these authentic tasks, students can demonstrate their ability to apply legal knowledge and skills in practical scenarios.

Online platforms

Leverage online platforms and technology to facilitate authentic assessments. Use LMSs and online assessment tools that allow students to submit their work electronically, receive timely feedback and engage in interactive assessment activities. Online platforms can also provide opportunities for collaborative assessments, such as group projects and peer reviews, fostering teamwork and enhancing the authenticity of the assessment process.

Timely feedback

Provide prompt and constructive feedback to students on their assessments. Feedback should not only focus on the final outcome but also highlight areas for improvement and offer guidance on how students can enhance their skills. Timely feedback enables students to reflect on their performance, identify strengths and weaknesses, and make necessary adjustments to their approach.

Formative and summative assessments

Incorporate both formative and summative assessments throughout the learning process. Formative assessments – such as quizzes, self-assessments and practice exercises – can allow students to receive ongoing feedback and monitor their progress. Summative assessments – such as examinations, research essays and oral presentations – can evaluate students' overall performance and mastery of the subject matter. By combining formative and summative assessments, students have opportunities to learn from their mistakes, refine their skills and demonstrate their competence in a comprehensive manner.

Rubrics and criteria

Develop clear assessment criteria and rubrics that align with the learning outcomes and authentic nature of the tasks. Clearly communicate expectations to students, outlining the specific knowledge, skills and qualities they should demonstrate in their assessments. Rubrics can help standardize the assessment process, promote fairness and provide students with a clear understanding of how their work will be evaluated.

Reflection and self-assessment

Encourage students to reflect on their assessments and engage in self-assessment. Promote metacognitive skills by prompting students to evaluate their own work, identify strengths and weaknesses, and set goals for improvement. Self-assessment enhances students' ability to evaluate their own performance critically and develop a deeper understanding of their learning progress.

*

By aligning assessments with the principles of authenticity, legal education can better prepare students for real-world legal practice. Through these assessments, students can gain practical experience, develop crucial legal skills and receive valuable feedback that supports their growth and development as legal professionals.

Continuous reflection and improvement

To ensure continuous reflection and improvement in legal education, legal educators should consider the following strategies.

Evaluation and feedback

Regularly evaluate the effectiveness of teaching methods and technology integration in legal education. Solicit feedback from students through surveys, focus groups and individual discussions to gather their perspectives on the learning experience. Pay attention to their suggestions, concerns and recommendations for improvement.

Self-reflective practice

Engage in personal reflection as an educator to critically assess your teaching methods, curriculum design and technology integration. Reflect on what worked well and what could be enhanced or modified to better meet the needs of students. Consider the impact of instructional strategies on student engagement, learning outcomes and overall satisfaction.

Professional development

Stay informed about advances in technology and pedagogy that are relevant to legal education. Attend conferences, workshops and webinars that focus on innovative teaching practices and emerging technologies. Engage in ongoing professional development to broaden your knowledge and acquire new skills that can enhance the learning experience for students.

Collaboration and sharing best practices

Collaborate with colleagues and participate in communities of practice to exchange ideas, share experiences and learn from one another. Discuss successful teaching methods, technology tools and instructional approaches that have proven effective in legal education. By collaborating with peers, you can gain valuable insights, gather diverse perspectives and identify strategies for improvement.

Continuous integration of technology

Stay updated on technological advances and evaluate their potential impact on legal education. Regularly explore new digital tools, platforms and resources that can enhance teaching and learning.

Embrace opportunities to integrate technology in ways that can promote active learning, engagement and accessibility for all students.

Pilot and experimentation

Adopt a mindset of experimentation and innovation. Pilot new teaching methods, technologies and instructional approaches on a small scale to assess their effectiveness before implementing them more widely. Use data and feedback from students to inform decisions about scaling up or refining these initiatives.

Collaboration with students

Involve students in the process of continuous improvement. Seek their input on instructional methods, technology integration and overall learning experience. Create opportunities for students to contribute to the design of the curriculum and suggest ways to enhance engagement and learning outcomes.

*

By embracing continuous reflection and improvement, legal educators can ensure that their teaching methods and technology integration remain effective, up-to-date and responsive to the evolving needs of students. Through ongoing evaluation, collaboration and professional development, legal education can continue to adapt and provide a high-quality learning experience for aspiring legal professionals.

Professional development

To support professional development in legal education, legal educators should consider the following strategies.

Digital literacy training

Provide instructors with training sessions and workshops focused on enhancing their digital literacy skills. Offer guidance on using specific tools, platforms and software relevant to legal education. Cover topics such as online teaching strategies, virtual collaboration, multimedia integration and assessment techniques using digital platforms.

Pedagogical training

Offer workshops and resources that focus on effective teaching strategies and instructional design principles. Provide guidance on creating engaging and interactive online learning experiences, fostering student engagement and promoting active learning. Equip tutors with the necessary skills to design and facilitate effective online discussions, group work and collaborative activities.

Technology integration support

Establish a support system that offers ongoing assistance and guidance to instructors as they integrate technology into their teaching practice. This can include dedicated technology support staff, instructional designers and peer mentors, all of whom can provide individualized guidance and troubleshooting. Create a repository of resources, tutorials and best practices that tutors can access for self-paced learning.

Collaborative learning communities

Foster collaboration and sharing of best practices among instructors. Establish a learning community or professional development groups in which tutors can share their experiences, insights and challenges related to technology integration. Encourage tutors to collaborate, discuss pedagogical strategies, exchange resources and provide peer feedback.

Guest speakers and expert presentations

Organize guest speaker sessions or invite experts in educational technology and digital learning to share their knowledge and experiences with instructors. These sessions can inspire instructors, provide them with new ideas and offer practical tips for effectively integrating technology into their teaching practice.

Reflective practice and action research

Encourage instructors to engage in reflective practice and action research to continuously improve their teaching methods. Encourage them to reflect on their teaching experiences, experiment with new approaches and assess the impact of technology integration on student learning outcomes. Promote the dissemination of research findings and encourage tutors to share their insights with the wider academic community.

Incentives and recognition

Recognize and reward instructors who demonstrate exemplary use of technology in their teaching practice. Provide incentives such as awards, grants or professional development opportunities for those who actively engage in technology integration and share their experiences with others.

*

By providing opportunities for professional development, digital literacy training and collaborative learning communities, legal education institutions can empower instructors to effectively integrate technology into their teaching practice. This support enables tutors to enhance their skills, stay current with emerging trends and continuously improve the learning experience for their students.

SUMMARY OF KEY MESSAGES

The principle of teaching that adapts to the environment can work in practice

- by embracing the use of online platforms, virtual classrooms and digital tools to create an interactive and engaging learning environment;

- by designing learning experiences that reflect real-world legal practice;
- by fostering active learning through encouraging student participation, discussion and collaboration;
- by emphasizing the ability to adapt to changing circumstances in legal practice;
- by aligning assessments with the principles of authentic assessment;
- by regularly reflecting on the effectiveness of teaching methods and technology integration; and
- by providing opportunities for tutors to enhance their digital literacy and teaching skills.

By incorporating these practical approaches, legal educators can create an adaptable and technology-enhanced learning environment that prepares students for the evolving legal landscape. This principle enables legal education to respond effectively to external factors, such as technological advancements and societal changes, ensuring graduates are equipped with the skills and competencies necessary for success in their legal careers.

There are some difficulties in implementing this principle, however, and addressing these requires a collaborative effort among legal educators, administrators and support staff. It involves providing the necessary resources, training and support to ensure successful adaptation to changing environments.

Additionally, continuous evaluation and improvement of teaching practices and support services are crucial to meet the evolving needs of students and to navigate future challenges.

HINTS AND TIPS

» ***Technological barriers.*** Implementing teaching practices that adapt to changing environments often involves the use of technology and online learning platforms. However, some students and tutors might not have access to reliable technology or the necessary digital literacy skills to effectively engage with these tools. Overcoming these technological barriers and ensuring equitable access to resources can be challenging.

» ***Training and support.*** Instructors may require training and support to effectively adapt their teaching methods to changing environments. They need to develop skills in using online platforms, creating engaging online learning experiences and effectively integrating technology into their pedagogical practices. Providing adequate training and ongoing support to tutors can be a time-consuming and resource-intensive process.

» ***Curriculum design and flexibility.*** Adapting teaching to changing environments requires a flexible curriculum that can accommodate unexpected disruptions and shifting priorities. Designing a curriculum that is adaptable and responsive to external factors such as health crises and technological advancements can be hard, requiring careful planning and continuous evaluation and adjustment.

» ***Maintaining engagement and motivation.*** In an online and rapidly changing environment, it can be challenging to maintain student engagement and motivation. Students may face distractions, technological difficulties or a sense of isolation. Legal educators need to employ innovative strategies to keep students engaged and motivated, such as incorporating interactive activities, fostering peer collaboration and providing timely feedback.

» ***Assessment and evaluation.*** Authentic assessment in a changing environment can be complex. Designing assessments that align with real-world legal practice and reflect the evolving demands of the profession requires careful consideration. Additionally, evaluating student performance and providing meaningful feedback in an online and changing environment can present challenges.

» ***Resource allocation.*** Adapting teaching to changing environments may require additional resources, such as technology infrastructure, software licences, and professional development opportunities. Institutions need to allocate resources effectively to support faculty members and students in adapting to new teaching methods and technologies.

» ***Student support and wellbeing.*** Adapting to changing environments can introduce additional stress and challenges for students. Institutions need to provide adequate support services to address students' wellbeing, support their mental health and help them navigate any specific challenges they may face during times of change.

CHAPTER 8

Responding to challenges of vocational pedagogies

This theme was based around teaching, learning, assessment and feedback, and it emerged in part out of some of the data relating to the codes for 'authentic assessment' and 'problem-based learning'. The data that particularly gave rise to this theme was that of participants giving examples of how they used the key aspects of authentic assessment and PBL – in terms of self-directed learning, collaboration and real-world relevance – as vocational pedagogies to teach legal skills to law students. There was plenty of evidence in the interviews of participants using authentic assessment and PBL for teaching legal skills in their modules, even though participants hardly ever used these specific terms to describe what they were doing. As demonstrated within the sub-codes of oral assessment, collaboration, guided PBL, group work and reflection, the examples given in interviews tended to accord quite closely with the requirements of authentic assessment and PBL.

One good example of authentic assessment that emerged from the data was that of Andrew's students collaborating in order to interview clients in the real-life setting of a law clinic, then reflecting on this experience afterwards in a journal. Another was Rick's extensive use of both formative and summative oral assessment in his modules.

A helpful illustration of the use of PBL in this study was Laura getting her students to do problem-based application work, which she said she tried to make as realistic and collaborative as possible. Jack also talked in his interview about using problem scenarios that assessed students' written skills and developed their powers of reasoning.

Perhaps most notably, participants seemed to regard actual real-world learning experiences as having the most value. However, simply making the experience realistic or as close to real life for the students as possible was still considered by law teachers to be effective. This seems to suggest that a realistic task or assessment, as opposed to an actual real-life one, may be sufficient for the purposes of achieving at least some of the benefits of authentic assessment, such as encouraging reflection and improving communication in students. Similarly, in the examples given above, there were still apparent benefits to be derived from PBL-type activity even where not all of the characteristics of this teaching method were present, such as students learning to work together in groups even if their learning was not always fully self-directed.

There was a departure, however, when it came to the challenges identified by academic opinion in comparison with the views of law teachers in this study. Namely, academic resistance (identified as a significant barrier to the implementation of authentic assessment[1]) did not seem to be a particular issue for participants, which was perhaps unsurprising since there was not a complete pedagogic transformation but only a few examples of authentic assessment and PBL-type activities in some modules. Instead, participants in interviews referred far more to student-centred problems. Above all other challenges, getting students to take a more self-directed approach to their own learning and approach to assessment, especially when those students came from widening participation backgrounds, was an issue identified by several law teachers. Given that the same participants spoke in very positive terms about the benefits of teaching and assessment approaches that made use of PBL and authentic assessment, recognizing and dealing with these challenges appears to be a worthy goal, and one that is worth prioritizing.

Taking all of this into account, this theme ultimately provided a starting point for consideration of another principle of authentic teaching and assessment practice for law, one that is centred on teaching to overcome the challenges of vocational pedagogies such as authentic assessment and PBL.

THE TEACHING TO OVERCOME CHALLENGES OF VOCATIONAL PEDAGOGIES PRINCIPLE

The principle of teaching to overcome challenges of vocational pedagogies was developed out of the theme of responding to challenges of vocational pedagogies. It tackles the challenges for law teachers in adapting their modules to incorporate authentic learning and assessment in preparing students for employment, with a particular focus on problems that affect students, such as directing their own learning.

This principle has most in common with the reason-based teaching element of the CARE framework, which discussed introducing legal reasoning to students. The pedagogy principle is, however, much wider in scope, as it is based around teaching, learning, assessment and feedback and was formed out of codes for 'authentic assessment' and 'PBL' through examples identified in the study of oral exercises, collaborative tasks, guided PBL, group work and reflection. That said, enhancement of students' legal reasoning, thinking and judgment is still very much at the heart of this principle, especially as this is a key element of authentic assessment that has been emphasized in the literature.

It has been suggested that authentic assessment should encourage students to engage with assessment criteria, judge their own performance and thereby regulate their learning. Evaluative judgment is particularly important for student learning because it promotes students' ability to judge the quality of their work and helps them to identify areas that need improvement, it tracks their progress over time, and it develop insights into acceptable standards of quality performance in their future profession.[2]

In terms of practical solutions and teaching interventions put forward through consideration of the perspectives of participants in this study, the focus within this principle is mainly on enhancement of formative assessment practices to take account of challenges faced by and from students, particularly getting them to engage with authentic assessment and PBL in order to improve their evaluative judgment capabilities.

One technique used to tackle these student-centred issues by a participant in my study was when Laura ensured that the problem-based work that she did with her students in seminars was as realistic as possible. Another was Derek getting his students to read real legal cases together in his workshops. Andrew made his students collaborate in mock interviews with each other, and Nora's students performed an advocacy exercise in an actual courtroom. This diverse range of formative assessment practices seems to reflect the recommended approach in the literature, i.e. that students need to be exposed to a variety of tasks and requirements and have plenty of opportunities to seek and engage in feedback about their workplace performance.[3]

There is also arguably a link here to supporting student resilience through self-regulated learning, as it has been suggested that effective feedback should enable learners to work towards self-regulated learning so that they can plan and manage the improvement of their own learning in the future.[4] This concept of self-regulated learning refers to the degree to which students can regulate aspects of their thinking, motivation and behaviour during learning, e.g. by setting learning goals and strategies for achieving them. This therefore has a great deal in common with the approach to formative authentic assessment, as it has been suggested that courses should use structured and varied feedback practices in order to develop self-regulated learning.[5]

Teaching to overcome challenges of vocational pedagogies is an extensive principle that covers several of the requirements for SQE candidates under the Statement. Legal reasoning and evaluative judgment are specifically recognized under the 'professionalism and judgment' requirement, which refers to recognizing and identifying ethical issues, relevant legal principles and rules of professional conduct, and exercising judgment in following them.

The technical legal practice requirement also recognizes the importance of evaluative judgment in undertaking legal research, and this is even highlighted under the requirement of working with others when it comes to 'understanding and responding effectively to clients' particular needs, objectives, priorities and constraints'.[6] As an element that supplements development of critical thinking and legal reasoning abilities in students, it is notable that the Statement also highlights reflection in terms of the need for students to reflect on and learn from practice as well as from others.

Enhancing students' problem-solving capabilities is also a key component of the law curriculum (see chapter 1), and illustrates a clear role for PBL in particular. This principle thus underscores the significance of legal reasoning, which it would therefore seem sensible to incorporate throughout the law degree, introducing students to problems that require reasoning skills for their solution at the earliest stage possible and then building on this with more advanced exercises that use realistic components such as interviews and advocacy as students progress through their studies.

HOW THE PRINCIPLE OF TEACHING TO OVERCOME CHALLENGES OF VOCATIONAL PEDAGOGIES CAN WORK IN PRACTICE

In practice, the principle of teaching to overcome challenges of vocational pedagogies can be implemented through various strategies and approaches. Some practical ways to apply this principle are listed below.

Authentic problem-based learning

Authentic PBL is a student-centred approach that places students in the role of legal practitioners faced with real-life challenges. To incorporate authentic PBL into the legal curriculum, legal educators should consider the following.

Real-life scenarios

Develop PBL scenarios that reflect the types of challenge encountered in legal practice. These scenarios can involve complex legal issues, conflicting interests and ethical dilemmas. Draw inspiration from actual legal cases or create hypothetical situations that closely resemble real-world legal problems.

Active learning

PBL requires students to engage actively in problem solving, critical thinking and legal analysis. Rather than receiving information passively, students become active participants in their own learning. They investigate the facts of the given case, research applicable laws and precedents, identify relevant legal principles and propose reasoned arguments and solutions.

Collaborative learning

Encourage students to work in teams or small groups to solve the PBL scenarios. Collaborative learning promotes the exchange of ideas, fosters diverse perspectives and strengthens teamwork and communication skills. Students can discuss different approaches, challenge assumptions and collectively develop comprehensive solutions.

Research and analysis

PBL requires students to conduct thorough research and analysis to understand the legal issues at hand. They should explore relevant statutes, regulations, case law, legal commentary and other authoritative sources. Encourage students to evaluate the credibility and relevance of sources critically, analyse conflicting viewpoints and integrate their findings into their problem-solving process.

Application of legal knowledge

PBL allows students to apply their legal knowledge in a practical context. They must identify the legal principles and rules that are most applicable to the given problem, analyse how these principles interact and determine how they should be applied to the specific case. This process helps students bridge the gap between legal theory and practice.

Reflection and evaluation

Integrate reflective practices throughout the PBL process. Encourage students to reflect on their problem-solving strategies, decision-making processes and the ethical implications of their proposed solutions. Provide opportunities for students to evaluate the strengths and weaknesses of their approaches and consider alternative perspectives.

Feedback and assessment

Provide timely and constructive feedback on students' problem-solving processes, legal analysis and proposed solutions. Assess their ability to apply legal reasoning, critical thinking and evaluative judgment in a real-world context. Offer both formative feedback during the PBL process and summative feedback for assessments to gauge students' mastery of the subject matter.

*

By incorporating authentic PBL into the legal curriculum, students are actively engaged in developing the skills and competencies required for legal practice. They can gain valuable experience in problem solving, legal analysis, teamwork and critical thinking, preparing them for the complexities and challenges they will face in their future legal careers.

Collaborative learning

Collaborative learning is an effective approach that fosters active student engagement, critical thinking and communication skills. To enhance collaborative learning experiences in the legal education setting, legal educators should consider the following strategies.

Group formation

Organize students into diverse groups or pairs, ensuring a mix of backgrounds, perspectives and skill sets. This promotes peer-to-peer learning and encourages students to challenge their own assumptions and consider alternative viewpoints.

Clear objectives

Clearly communicate the learning objectives and expectations for the collaborative tasks. This helps students understand the purpose of their collaboration and align their efforts towards achieving the desired outcomes.

Structured activities

Design structured activities that require students to participate actively and contribute to the group's work. For example, students can engage in case analysis, where each group member is assigned a specific aspect of the case to research and analyse. They can then come together to share their findings, discuss the legal issues and develop a comprehensive analysis collectively.

Role assignments

Assign specific roles and responsibilities to each group member to promote equal participation and accountability. For instance, one student can be designated as the group facilitator, responsible for managing discussions and keeping the group on track, while another student can serve as the researcher, responsible for gathering relevant legal information.

Effective communication

Encourage students to engage in effective communication within their groups. This includes active listening, asking clarifying questions and providing constructive feedback to one another. Students should be encouraged to express their ideas, challenge assumptions and engage in respectful debates to deepen their understanding of legal concepts and issues.

Reflection and debriefing

Provide opportunities for groups to reflect on their collaborative experiences. After completing a task, allow time for groups to discuss what worked well, what challenges they encountered and how they could improve their collaboration in the future. Facilitate a debriefing session where groups can share their insights and lessons learned with the whole class.

Assessing individual and group performance

Consider both individual and group assessments to ensure fairness and recognize individual contributions to the collaborative learning process. Individual assessments can include self-reflections, peer evaluations or written reflections on the group work. Group assessments can focus on the quality of the group's work, their ability to work cohesively and their collective problem-solving skills.

*

By fostering collaborative learning experiences, students develop not only legal knowledge but also teamwork, communication and critical-thinking skills that are crucial in legal practice. They can learn to collaborate effectively with others, consider multiple perspectives and arrive at reasoned judgments collectively – a reflection of the collaborative nature of legal work.

Formative assessment

Formative assessment plays a crucial role in supporting students' learning and growth throughout their legal education journey. To incorporate formative assessment methods effectively, legal educators should consider the following approaches.

Ongoing feedback

Provide regular and timely feedback on students' work, highlighting both strengths and areas for improvement. Offer specific and constructive comments that focus on students' legal reasoning, analytical skills and evaluative judgment. Encourage students to reflect on the feedback and use it to guide their learning process.

Self-assessment

Promote self-assessment by encouraging students to evaluate their own work critically. Provide them with rubrics, checklists and guiding questions that help them to assess their legal analysis, research skills and the effectiveness of their written and oral arguments.

Encourage students to set goals for improvement based on their self-assessment.

Peer assessment

Incorporate peer-assessment activities in which students evaluate and provide feedback on each other's work. This helps students not only to develop a deeper understanding of legal concepts by analysing their peers' work critically, but also by enhancing their ability to provide constructive feedback. Establish clear criteria and guidelines for peer assessment to ensure fairness and consistency.

Reflective journals or portfolios

Introduce reflective journals and portfolios in which students document their learning experiences, track their progress and reflect on their growth as legal practitioners. Encourage students to write reflections on their legal reasoning, their problem-solving strategies and the impact of feedback on their development. These reflective exercises can promote metacognition and deepen students' understanding of their learning process.

In-class quizzes and discussions

Use in-class quizzes and discussions to assess students' understanding of legal concepts, their ability to apply legal principles to real-world scenarios, and their critical-thinking skills. These activities can provide immediate feedback to students and allow instructors to identify areas where students may need additional support and clarification.

Revision and iterative feedback

Encourage students to revise and refine their work based on the feedback received. Offer opportunities for iterative feedback, allowing students to submit multiple drafts and engage in iterative problem-solving activities. This process encourages students to engage with feedback actively, make improvements and develop a deeper understanding of legal concepts and skills.

Individualized support

Provide individualized support to students who may require additional assistance or guidance. Offer office hours, tutorials and online consultations where students can seek clarification, ask questions and receive personalized feedback on their progress.

*

Incorporating formative assessment methods gives students the opportunity to receive feedback and guidance that supports their growth as legal professionals. They can develop self-assessment skills, enhance their ability to provide constructive feedback to others, and engage actively in their own learning process, ultimately improving their legal reasoning, evaluative judgment and overall performance in legal practice.

Authentic assessment tasks

Authentic assessment tasks are essential for preparing students for the challenges they will face in real-world legal practice. When designing these tasks, legal educators should consider the following approaches.

Oral exercises

Incorporate oral exercises – such as moot court competitions, client interviews and oral arguments – to assess students' ability to communicate effectively, think on their feet and present their legal analysis persuasively. These tasks can simulate the dynamic nature of legal practice and help students develop their oral advocacy skills.

Written assignments

Design written assignments that mirror the types of documents commonly used in legal practice, such as legal memoranda, briefs, contracts and opinions. These assignments assess students' ability to conduct thorough legal research, analyse complex legal issues and present their findings in a clear and concise manner.

Presentations

Include presentation tasks in which students present their legal analysis, arguments and solutions to a specific legal problem. This allows students to showcase their public speaking skills, demonstrate their understanding of legal concepts and communicate their ideas to a professional audience effectively.

Simulations and role plays

Use simulations and role plays to assess students' ability to navigate real-life legal scenarios. These can involve simulated negotiations, mediations and client counselling sessions. By participating in these activities, students can develop their problem-solving skills, negotiation tactics and client-management abilities.

Clear assessment criteria and rubrics

Provide students with clear assessment criteria and rubrics that outline the expectations for each task. These criteria should focus on legal reasoning, critical analysis, evaluative judgment and ethical considerations. Clearly communicate the weighting assigned to each criterion and provide examples of exemplary work to guide students' understanding of expectations.

Realistic context and authentic resources

Design assessment tasks that align with real-world legal practice. Situate assessment tasks within realistic legal contexts, incorporating relevant statutes, case law and professional guidelines. Provide students with access to authentic legal resources and research databases to support their analysis and decision making.

Ethical considerations

Incorporate ethical considerations into assessment tasks to evaluate students' understanding of legal ethics and professional responsibility. Assess their ability to identify and address ethical dilemmas that may arise in legal practice, emphasizing the importance of ethical decision making and professional conduct.

Peer assessment and self-assessment

Integrate peer-assessment and self-assessment components into the authentic assessment tasks. Encourage students to evaluate their own work and the work of their peers using the provided criteria and rubrics. Peer assessment and self-assessment can promote self-reflection, peer learning and the development of evaluative judgment skills..

*

Designing authentic assessment tasks gives students the opportunity to demonstrate their ability to apply legal knowledge, think critically, analyse complex legal issues and make sound decisions within a professional context. These tasks can provide valuable feedback to both students and instructors, helping students develop the skills necessary for success in the legal profession.

Reflection and metacognition

Reflection and metacognition play a crucial role in deepening students' understanding and enhancing their learning experiences. When incorporating reflection activities, legal educators should consider the following strategies.

Journals and learning logs

Assign regular journal entries where students can reflect on their learning, document challenges faced and identify strategies for improvement. Encourage them to express their thoughts, questions and insights related to their legal studies and practical experiences.

Group discussions and debriefing sessions

Organize group discussions and debriefing sessions during which students can share their experiences, discuss their approaches to solving legal problems and reflect on the outcomes. These discussions can provide an opportunity for students to learn from each other, gain different perspectives and refine their thinking processes.

Online reflection platforms

Use online platforms and learning management systems that facilitate reflection and metacognition. These platforms can include discussion boards, reflective journals and online surveys, all of which can prompt students to reflect on their learning journey, the challenges they have encountered and the strategies they have employed.

Guided reflection prompts

Provide guided reflection prompts that encourage students to think deeply about their learning experiences. Prompt them to consider what they learned, how they applied legal concepts and what strategies were effective or ineffective. Encourage them to reflect on their decision-making processes, evaluate the impact of their actions and identify areas for improvement.

Metacognitive strategies

Teach students metacognitive strategies, such as setting goals, monitoring their progress and evaluating their understanding. Prompt them to think about their thinking (metacognition) by asking questions such as 'What did I learn from this experience?' or 'How did I approach this problem, and what could I do differently next time?'

Reflective assessment tasks

Integrate reflective components into assessment tasks, where students are asked to analyse their learning process, evaluate their strengths and weaknesses, and propose strategies for improvement. This encourages students to engage in metacognitive thinking while demonstrating their understanding of legal concepts and skills.

Instructor feedback

Provide constructive feedback on students' reflections to guide their metacognitive development. Acknowledge their insights, ask probing questions and offer suggestions for further reflection and improvement. Use the feedback as an opportunity to encourage students' critical thinking and metacognitive awareness.

*

By incorporating reflection and metacognition into the learning process, students can develop a deeper understanding of their own learning and problem-solving approaches. They become more self-aware, adaptable and capable of identifying and addressing their own learning needs. These reflective practices can foster continuous improvement and empower students to take ownership of their learning in the legal field.

Professional skills development

Professional skills development is a crucial component of legal education, and it is essential to offer diverse opportunities for students to develop and practice these skills. Legal educators should consider the following strategies to foster the development of professional skills.

Legal-writing exercises

Incorporate legal-writing assignments that simulate real-world scenarios, such as drafting memoranda, briefs, contracts and legal opinions. Provide clear guidelines and feedback to help students refine their writing skills, legal analysis and effective communication.

Negotiation simulations

Organize negotiation exercises during which students can practise their negotiation skills in a controlled environment. Assign students different roles, such as solicitors and clients, and provide scenarios that require them to negotiate and reach mutually beneficial outcomes. Provide feedback on their negotiation strategies, problem-solving abilities and communication skills.

Client interviews

Arrange opportunities for students to conduct mock client interviews. These exercises can allow students to practise active listening, empathy and effective communication with clients. Provide feedback on their ability to gather relevant information, identify legal issues and build rapport with clients.

Mooting competitions

Encourage students to participate in mooting competitions, where they can argue hypothetical cases in front of judges or experienced practitioners. Mooting competitions can provide valuable experience in legal research, oral advocacy and critical thinking. Offer coaching and feedback to help students refine their argumentation and presentation skills.

Courtroom advocacy exercises

Organize courtroom advocacy exercises that simulate real courtroom settings. Students can engage in mock trials, presenting arguments and examining witnesses. These exercises can develop students' oral advocacy skills, courtroom etiquette and ability to think on their feet.

Professionalism and ethics training

Offer workshops and seminars on professional ethics and conduct. Provide students with guidance on ethical dilemmas they may encounter in legal practice and help them to develop the skills needed to navigate these situations responsibly.

Legal research and analysis

Incorporate activities that allow students to develop and refine their legal research and analytical skills. Provide assignments that require students to identify relevant legal sources, analyse legal issues and apply legal principles to practical scenarios. Offer feedback on their research strategies, critical thinking and ability to support their legal arguments effectively.

Experiential learning opportunities

Facilitate internships, placements and clinical programmes that provide students with real-world experience working in legal settings. These opportunities can allow students to apply their legal knowledge and skills in a practical context, while receiving supervision and feedback from experienced professionals.

*

By being offered a range of professional skills development activities, students can gain practical experience, refine their legal skills and develop the critical thinking and professional judgment necessary for success in legal practice. These hands-on experiences can complement theoretical knowledge and help students bridge the gap between the classroom and the real-world legal environment.

Training and support

Training and support are essential components of implementing effective pedagogical approaches and tools associated with authentic learning and assessment strategies. Legal educators should consider the following strategies to provide training and support to both tutors and students.

Educator professional development

Offer professional development workshops, seminars and training sessions for instructors to enhance their understanding and implementation of authentic learning and assessment strategies. These sessions can provide tutors with insights into designing authentic assessments, integrating real-world scenarios into the curriculum and using feedback effectively. Provide resources, case studies and examples to demonstrate best practices, and encourage tutors to reflect on their teaching methods.

Faculty collaboration and sharing

Encourage collaboration among instructors by establishing platforms for sharing experiences, insights and resources related to implementing authentic learning and assessment strategies. This can include faculty meetings, online discussion forums or communities of practice. Foster a culture of sharing and continuous learning, where tutors can exchange ideas, troubleshoot challenges and inspire one another with innovative approaches.

Student orientation and training

Provide students with orientation sessions that introduce them to the principles and expectations of authentic learning and assessment. Teach students how to engage in self-regulated learning, access relevant resources and use feedback effectively to improve their legal reasoning and evaluative judgment skills. Offer workshops and tutorials on legal research, critical analysis and effective communication to support students in developing the necessary skills for authentic learning.

Peer support and mentoring

Facilitate peer-mentoring programmes where more experienced students can provide guidance and support to their peers. Pairing students at different stages of their legal education allows for the transfer of knowledge and the sharing of experiences, and it facilitates peer-to-peer feedback on legal reasoning and evaluative judgment skills. Provide training and resources to student mentors to enhance their mentoring skills and ensure a supportive learning community.

Online learning resources

Develop and provide online learning resources, such as video tutorials, interactive modules and self-paced courses, which address the principles and practices of authentic learning and assessment. These resources can be accessible to both instructors and students, serving as a reference guide and offering just-in-time support.

Academic support services

Collaborate with academic support services within the institution, such as learning centres or writing centres, to provide additional support to students. These services can offer workshops, individual consultations and tutoring sessions focused on legal reasoning, critical thinking and evaluative judgment skills. Ensure that students are aware of these resources and actively encourage their use.

Ongoing feedback and reflection

Encourage ongoing feedback and reflection from both educators and students on the effectiveness of the implemented strategies. Conduct regular evaluations, surveys and focus groups to gather input and insights from stakeholders. Use this feedback to refine and improve training and support initiatives, ensuring they address the evolving needs of instructors and students.

*

By providing comprehensive training and support to both instructors and students, institutions can foster an environment that promotes effective implementation of authentic learning and assessment strategies. This support enables educators to enhance their instructional practices and empowers students to develop and refine their legal reasoning and evaluative judgment skills.

SUMMARY OF KEY MESSAGES

The principle of teaching to overcome challenges of vocational pedagogies can work in practice

- by incorporating into the curriculum authentic and real-life problems that require students to apply legal reasoning, critical thinking and evaluative judgment;
- by fostering collaborative learning experiences in which students work together in groups or pairs to solve legal problems;
- by using formative assessment methods to support students' learning and development;
- by designing assessment tasks that align with real-world legal practice;
- by integrating reflection activities into the learning process, allowing students to think deeply about their learning experiences, the challenges they have encountered and the strategies they have employed;
- by offering opportunities for students to develop and practice essential professional skills; and
- by providing training and support to both instructors and students in using the pedagogical approaches and tools associated with this principle.

By implementing these strategies, legal educators can create an engaging and supportive learning environment that addresses the challenges of vocational pedagogies. Students will have opportunities to develop their legal reasoning abilities, enhance their evaluative judgment skills and prepare themselves effectively for future legal practice.

However, addressing some of the challenges of implementing this principle requires a comprehensive and collaborative approach that involves tutors, administrators and relevant stakeholders. This requires ongoing evaluation and refinement of teaching practices, alignment with learning outcomes and professional requirements, and a commitment to providing students with meaningful and relevant learning experiences that prepare them for employment in the legal profession.

> HINTS AND TIPS
>
> » *Integration of authentic learning and assessment.* Incorporating authentic learning and assessment in vocational pedagogies can be challenging. Designing and implementing activities that mirror real-world legal practice requires careful planning and alignment with learning outcomes. Ensuring that students have meaningful opportunities to apply legal reasoning, exercise evaluative judgment and develop problem-solving skills can be a complex task.
> » *Student engagement and motivation.* Encouraging students to direct their own learning and engage actively with authentic assessment and PBL can be difficult. Some students may struggle with self-regulated learning or may not see the immediate relevance of these approaches. Educators need to employ strategies to motivate and engage students, such as providing clear explanations of the benefits, offering support and guidance, and creating authentic and meaningful learning experiences.
> » *Assessment of evaluative judgment.* Assessing students' evaluative judgment capabilities can be demanding. Authentic assessment tasks that require students to judge the quality of their work and make improvements can be subjective and context dependent. Developing reliable and valid assessment criteria for evaluative judgment and providing effective feedback to support student learning and improvement requires careful consideration.
> » *Access to realistic learning experiences.* Providing students with access to realistic learning experiences, such as reading real legal cases and participating in mock interviews, can be challenging. It may require collaboration with external stakeholders, the securing of resources and ensuring that students have the necessary support and guidance to navigate these experiences effectively.
> » *Faculty development and support.* Adapting vocational pedagogies and incorporating authentic learning and assessment approaches may require faculty development and support. Instructors need opportunities for professional development to enhance

their knowledge and skills in designing and implementing these pedagogical practices. Institutions need to provide resources, training and ongoing support to faculty members to ensure effective implementation.

» *Curriculum design and coordination.* Developing a coherent and integrated curriculum that incorporates authentic learning and assessment can be a complex task. It requires careful coordination among different courses and modules to ensure that learning experiences and assessment tasks align and build upon each other. Curriculum mapping, collaboration among faculty members, and ongoing evaluation and improvement are essential.

» *Institutional support and recognition.* Institutions need to provide support and recognition for the implementation of vocational pedagogies that overcome challenges. This includes allocating resources, promoting a culture of innovation and continuous improvement, and recognizing and rewarding faculty members' efforts to incorporate authentic learning and assessment approaches.

CHAPTER 9

Integrating academic skills and vocational skills

This theme focuses on the skills, both soft and hard, that law teachers consider students need to acquire, and more specifically on the tension between these soft and hard skills on the one hand, and on the blurring of the distinction between academic skills and vocational skills on the other. As such, this theme partly developed out of thematic links between the codes for 'vocational legal skills' and 'academic legal skills' in the data.

My study's participants seemed to be more comfortable talking about academic legal skills rather than vocational legal skills, and more examples of the former were provided in the interviews. These included setting legal referencing tasks for students, in Tracy's case, and coming up with problem scenarios, used by Jack to assess his students' written skills and develop their powers of reasoning.

When vocational skills, such as interpersonal skills, were mentioned in the data, it was usually in terms of a recent change to the way that legal skills teaching was being delivered. Additionally, it was mostly the participants with a previous background in legal practice that were more keen to talk about how they were adapting their teaching to this change. For example, Ray talked about developing students' commercial awareness by mentioning this aspect specifically in his sessions; Nora got her students to produce skeleton arguments for mock trials as a form of formative assessment that reflected practice; and Rick made his students do oral presentations in class in order to improve their confidence and public-speaking skills.

Even where vocational skills were discussed, it was often in the context of formative rather than summative assessment. To offset this, while participants seemed to find more traditional academic legal skills to be within their comfort zone, such as legal research or reasoning, even those with no background in legal practice took pains to relate skills teaching in some way to what professional lawyers did through authentic teaching and assessment. An example of this was Derek (a career academic with no prior experience of professional practice) running workshops that focused on critical thinking and critical reading of legal texts but getting students to collaborate in so doing. This way of working was designed to simulate collaborating with colleagues in an office environment.

While there are parallels between this theme and the practice theme, the two do capture distinct aspects of the data and represent different concepts within it. The practice theme is concerned specifically with preparing students for professional legal practice, and as such it relates to data about the challenges of the practice of law as a professional career. The skills theme, on the other hand, looks more at the tension between academic and vocational skills and at how participants have reconciled this tension.

To emphasize the blurring of the lines between vocational and academic skills, there was data suggesting that there are law teachers who do not see any distinction at all between the two. Both Bob and Laura, for example, said that the distinction was either not useful or that they simply did not recognize it. This ties in with the literature (see chapter 1) and lends support to the idea that the so-called liberal/vocational divide in legal education, i.e. the balance between the academic and vocational content of the law curriculum, may be overstated.

Laura provided one of the most notable answers to the question of what standard of work students produced in legal skills tasks, as compared with more abstract theoretical tasks like essays, when she stated that she did not recognize any distinction between legal skills assessment tasks and theoretical legal assessment tasks. Laura felt that this was an important point to make regarding this issue, i.e. that there was not an uncontested distinction between legal-theory-based and legal-skills-based assessment, especially as making such a distinction appeared to downgrade both types of assessment in her view. Having said this, Laura then went on to say that, while some students did seem to prefer, and do better in, what might be regarded as more practice-based or advice-based assessments, this very much depended on the student. Laura's comments make clear that not all law teachers see any such distinction between the academic and vocational content of the law curriculum. This strengthens the view that this might be a false dichotomy.

When responding to my final interview question – whether there was anything else to add that had not been covered but that might be relevant – Bob made a point that supported Laura's comments. It was notable, I think, that Bob felt that making this point was important enough to merit a separate answer to a free-standing question given that he had not spoken about this issue prior to that point in his interview. Like Laura, Bob had emphasized the importance of teaching legal skills throughout his interview, as well as discussing his personal experience of teaching them during his career as a lecturer. As noted, this also seemed to endorse Laura's view that the concept of a distinction between legal skills and substantive law modules was neither accurate nor helpful.

This also links in with a point made in the literature review about how skills cannot easily be taught in isolation from the rest of the programme. Indeed, the comments made by participants as referred to here raises questions about the extent to which teaching skills in separate modules could be regarded as authentic teaching and assessment unless they are linked to real-life cases – an issue that was explored further under the pedagogy theme.

There was certainly no evidence in my study of rival camps of academics, divided between those committed to a liberal education and others on the side of a vocational one. The tension, if it existed at all, was more in terms of law teachers accepting the need to change and adapt to new practices in teaching and assessment in order to better prepare students with the sorts of skills that they would need in their future careers, whether academic or vocational, and trying to work out the best way to do this.

What became clear, however, was that while the traditional academic legal skills were familiar to participants and appeared well embedded in the legal curriculum, the vocational aspect had not yet been fully introduced and was to some extent still under development. Recent events – such as changes in the profession, discussed more under the practice theme, and the effect of the pandemic, as discussed within the environment theme – seemed to have accelerated the shift to a more vocational pedagogy when it came to legal skills, or at least heightened awareness of this aspect. This theme therefore shows what came out of my research in terms of a particular set of data. It also offers the potential to be developed into a principle based around teaching to integrate academic and vocational skills in order to better incorporate authentic assessment and PBL into legal education.

THE TEACHING TO INTEGRATE ACADEMIC AND VOCATIONAL SKILLS PRINCIPLE

The principle of teaching to integrate academic and vocational skills – which came out of the integrating academic skills and vocational skills theme and also brought together the separate codes on 'academic legal skills' and 'vocational legal skills' – emphasizes the importance of law teachers, relating their legal skills teaching to the behaviour of professional lawyers through authentic teaching and assessment.

In relation to the CARE framework,[1] this principle aligns most closely with 'empathetic teaching', which is about teachers communicating non-verbally with their students, although this goes beyond collaborative work, mentoring and student law clinics to also embrace what may be regarded as more traditional academic legal skills, such as legal research and reasoning.

In my study, while participants seemed to find these traditional academic legal skills to be within their comfort zone, even those with no background in legal practice took pains to relate what they were doing in the classroom in some way to what professional lawyers did in practice through authentic teaching and assessment, as demonstrated through the sub-codes relating to adapting to change, formative assessment, legal drafting and summative assessment. This principle also builds on the relevant literature, which indicates that authentic assessment tasks should provide students with opportunities to take on roles as legal professionals and reflect upon this, thus straddling the roles of student and future practitioner, in order to develop their understanding of what it means to fit in with workplace practices and thereby take the first steps to achieving success in their chosen profession.[2]

Empathetic teaching is also connected with emotion management, and, indeed, a significant focus of Tsaoussi's CARE framework is on bringing an understanding of the affective domain into legal education. The affective domain involves the study of how emotions are expressed and learned, how they arise and how they are experienced, what they are influenced by and how they influence behaviour. Taking emotion into account is critical for the teaching process, but the affective domain has been largely ignored in legal education, especially at the curriculum design level.[3] The significance of this is that unless law teachers engage with the motivations and emotional experiences of their students, those students will not care about what they are learning or its consequences. Engaging well with affect in legal education can therefore have a positive impact on both the behaviour and the performance of students, while ignoring the affective domain risks students losing both confidence and interest in their studies.

There is a case for rethinking curriculum design in light of this, and there are a number of ways of embedding affect in the curriculum. For example, Tsaoussi refers to good classroom management to create a safe and supportive environment for students, particularly when it comes to negotiation, and this is borne out to some extent by Tracy's comments in my study that it was crucial for her students to learn that the point of negotiation was not simply to batter the other party into submission but to encourage the more positive elements that they enjoyed, like teamwork. More generally, therefore, affect may be embedded in the curriculum by creating more space for student dialogue and creativity.

The data within the skills theme also highlighted, however, that while more traditional academic legal skills were familiar to participants and appeared to be well embedded in the legal curriculum, the vocational aspect had not yet been fully introduced and was to some extent still under development. When vocational skills, such as interpersonal skills, were discussed, it was usually in terms of a recent change to the way that legal skills teaching was being delivered, and it was often in the context of formative rather than summative assessment. Nevertheless, there was a universal acceptance among participants of the need to change and to adapt to new practices in teaching and assessment in order to better prepare students with the sorts of skills that they would need in their future careers.

Examples in my research of participants working out the best way to accomplish this goal provide useful suggestions to incorporate into teaching and assessment practices more generally. Andrew, for instance, indicated that in his module the development of vocational skills in law students was directly linked to preparation for summative assessment. In this way, simulations of trials, meetings with clients and the writing of client letters, all of which were formative, were in fact part of a continual learning process, in that they were all subsequently used by students as part of their reflective portfolios, which were the summative assessment in Andrew's module.

Such authentic assessment tasks thus have the potential to demonstrate to students that legal skills are essentially about how they apply in practice what they learn at law school. There is still some way to go in this area, however: it was clear from my study that, while the more traditional academic legal skills were familiar to participants and appeared to be well embedded in the legal curriculum, the vocational aspect was to an extent still a work in progress. This is therefore clearly an endeavour that is not without its challenges, particularly for those who may not have had previous experience of professional practice, thus reinforcing the need for adequate support and training for law teachers.

While the skills principle recognizes the importance of enhancing students' personal and interpersonal attributes, it also returns the focus to enhancement of field-specific knowledge and skills, as well as more generic skills. With its emphasis on integrating vocational and academic skills, this principle maps closely onto the Statement's requirements for professionalism and judgment, and is closely associated with the technical legal practice aspect for SQE candidates. Under both requirements, while traditional academic skills like undertaking legal research, applying legal principles to factual issues, and using clear and accurate language are mentioned, equal significance is attached to more vocationally relevant aspects such as 'disclosing when work is beyond their personal capability', 'knowing when to seek expert advice' and 'identifying all parties' interests, objectives and limits'.[4] Clearly, incorporation of the latter elements into law modules will only be possible through simulation of realistic work-based classroom tasks and assessments.

While many aspects of teaching law are best demonstrated by example, whether in the form of model answers or guides to best practice, when it comes to vocational elements this need to illustrate to students the standard to which they should be aiming is only amplified. In a professional workplace setting it is often only through experience and the example provided by more experienced colleagues that knowing when to seek expert advice, for instance, will be learned – similar room needs to be found in the law curriculum for these sorts of lesson to be imparted to students.

HOW THE PRINCIPLE OF TEACHING TO INTEGRATE ACADEMIC AND VOCATIONAL SKILLS CAN WORK IN PRACTICE

Implementing the principle of teaching to integrate academic and vocational skills in practice involves several strategies, as set out below.

Authentic teaching and assessment

Authentic teaching and assessment are crucial elements in preparing students for real-world legal practice. Some ways of implementing this principle are given below.

Simulations and role plays

Incorporate simulations and role plays that simulate real-world legal scenarios. These activities can involve mock trials, client interviews, negotiations and legal drafting exercises. By engaging in these simulations, students can develop practical skills and gain experience in applying legal knowledge to authentic situations. Provide students with detailed scenarios, roles and relevant background information to make the simulations as realistic as possible.

Case studies and problem-solving tasks

Integrate case studies and problem-solving tasks that reflect the complexities and challenges of legal practice into the curriculum. Present students with real or hypothetical legal cases that require them to analyse facts, identify legal issues, research applicable laws and propose solutions. These activities can foster critical thinking, legal reasoning and the application of legal principles to practical situations.

Client engagement

Create opportunities for students to engage with clients through supervised interactions. This can involve conducting client interviews and counselling sessions and participating in legal clinics. Through these experiences, students can develop communication and interpersonal skills, learn to address client needs and concerns, and navigate ethical dilemmas. Faculty supervision and feedback ensures that students receive guidance and support throughout the client engagement process.

Legal drafting and document preparation

Incorporate assignments that require students to draft legal documents, such as contracts, memoranda, pleadings and opinions. Provide clear guidelines and templates so that students can familiarize themselves with the format, style and language used in legal practice. Review and provide feedback on students' drafts, focusing on clarity, organization, legal analysis and adherence to professional standards.

Feedback and assessment

Provide feedback and assessment criteria that align with professional expectations and standards. Use rubrics and guidelines to evaluate students' performance in authentic tasks, focusing on their legal reasoning, analytical skills, professional judgment and ethical considerations. Provide timely and constructive feedback that helps students to understand their strengths and areas for improvement. Incorporate self-assessment and peer-assessment activities to encourage students to reflect on their work and provide feedback to their peers.

Industry practitioners as guest speakers

Invite legal professionals to share their experiences, insights and expertise through guest lectures and panel discussions. These practitioners can provide first-hand knowledge of the realities of legal practice, share practical tips and offer guidance on professional development. Engage students in Q&A sessions to facilitate direct interaction with industry experts.

Professional ethics and standards

Incorporate discussions and activities that emphasize professional ethics and the importance of upholding ethical standards in legal practice. Explore case studies and hypothetical scenarios that raise ethical dilemmas and require students to analyse and reflect, and then to propose ethical solutions. This cultivates students' ethical awareness and prepares them to navigate complex ethical challenges they may encounter in their careers.

*

By designing authentic teaching and assessment strategies, legal educators can provide students with a realistic and immersive learning experience. These activities enable students to develop the skills, knowledge and professionalism required to succeed in the legal profession. Additionally, aligning feedback and assessment with professional expectations ensures that students receive meaningful guidance and can improve their performance continuously.

Relating to professional behaviour

Relating to professional behaviour is an essential aspect of legal education. Some ways to expand on this principle are listed below.

Ethics and professional responsibility

Integrate discussions and activities that focus on legal ethics and professional responsibility. Explore the rules and codes of conduct that govern lawyers' behaviour, and discuss the ethical dilemmas they may face in practice. Use case studies, scenarios and hypothetical situations to prompt students to analyse ethical issues, consider multiple perspectives and make reasoned judgments. Encourage students to reflect on their own values and their ethical decision-making processes.

Effective communication

Emphasize the importance of effective communication skills in legal practice. Provide opportunities for students to practise written and oral communication in a legal context. Assign tasks such as drafting persuasive arguments, presenting oral arguments and participating in mock negotiations. Provide constructive feedback on students' communication skills, including their clarity, organization, persuasiveness and professionalism. Discuss the role of effective communication in building client relationships, collaborating with colleagues and advocating for clients' interests.

Professionalism and work etiquette

Educate students on the expectations and behaviour of professional lawyers. Discuss topics such as punctuality, professional appearance, ethical behaviour and maintaining client confidentiality. Explore the importance of professionalism in building a reputable legal career and fostering trust with clients and colleagues. Engage students in activities that simulate professional interactions, such as client interviews, team meetings and negotiation exercises, and provide feedback on their professionalism and work etiquette.

Reflective practice

Encourage students to engage in reflective practice to develop self-awareness and enhance their professional development. Provide opportunities for students to reflect on their own behaviours, strengths and areas for improvement. Encourage them to set goals for professional growth and develop strategies to achieve those goals. Incorporate reflective exercises, such as journaling, self-assessment and group discussions, to facilitate this process.

Professional role models

Invite legal professionals from diverse backgrounds to share their experiences and insights with students. These professionals can serve as role models and mentors, providing guidance on professional behaviour, career development and navigating the legal profession. Arrange networking events, mentoring programmes and guest speaker sessions during which students can interact with these professionals and gain valuable insights.

Case studies on professional conduct

Analyse real-life examples of professional conduct, both positive and negative, to illustrate the importance of ethical behaviour and professional standards. Discuss landmark cases, disciplinary proceedings and ethical controversies to help students understand the consequences of ethical violations and their impact on the legal profession. Engage students in discussions and debates about the ethical implications of various actions and decisions.

*

By connecting legal skills teaching to the practical aspects of legal practice and by emphasising professionalism, ethics and effective communication, legal educators can help students develop the behaviours and mindset necessary for a successful legal career. Through reflection, analysis of professional conduct and exposure to professional role models, students can gain a deeper understanding of the expectations and responsibilities associated with being a professional lawyer.

Embedding the affective domain

Embedding the affective domain in legal education is crucial for supporting students' holistic development and fostering a positive learning experience. Some ways to expand on this principle are given below.

An emotionally supportive environment

Create a classroom environment that promotes emotional wellbeing and inclusivity. Encourage open and respectful dialogue, where students feel comfortable expressing their thoughts, concerns and perspectives. Foster a sense of belonging by valuing and acknowledging students' diverse experiences and backgrounds. Incorporate activities that can promote empathy and understanding, such as group discussions, collaborative projects and storytelling exercises.

Self-reflection and self-awareness

Integrate opportunities for students to engage in self-reflection and develop self-awareness. Encourage students to reflect on their own emotions, motivations and learning experiences. Assign reflective writing exercises, journaling activities and self-assessment tasks that can prompt students to consider their strengths, the challenges they face and their personal growth. Provide guidance and support for students to develop strategies for self-regulated learning and emotional wellbeing.

Peer feedback and support

Promote a culture of peer feedback and support within the classroom. Encourage students to provide constructive feedback to their peers, fostering a sense of collective growth and collaboration. Assign group projects and activities that can require students to work together, share ideas and offer feedback. Facilitate peer discussions and encourage students to listen actively and respond to each other's perspectives.

Personalized learning

Recognize and value the individual experiences, interests and aspirations of students. Provide opportunities for students to connect their personal experiences to the content being taught. Incorporate examples and case studies that can resonate with students' backgrounds and interests. Encourage creativity and allow for student choice and autonomy in assignments and projects, fostering a sense of ownership and motivation.

Experiential learning and real-world connections

Engage students in experiential learning activities that connect legal concepts to real-world situations. Provide opportunities for students to apply their knowledge and skills in authentic contexts. Incorporate case studies, simulations and practical exercises that can mirror the complexities of legal practice. Encourage students to reflect on the emotional and ethical dimensions of legal issues and consider the impact of their decisions on different stakeholders.

Mindfulness and wellbeing

Introduce mindfulness practices and wellbeing strategies to support students' emotional resilience and stress management. Incorporate brief mindfulness exercises, breathing techniques and relaxation activities at the beginning or end of class to promote a sense of calm and focus. Share resources on stress reduction, time management and self-care to support students' overall wellbeing.

*

By embedding the affective domain in legal education, legal educators can create an inclusive and supportive learning environment in which students' emotions, motivations and experiences are acknowledged and valued. This approach promotes personal growth, resilience and deeper engagement with the subject matter. It also prepares students for navigating the emotional complexities of legal practice and helps them develop the empathy and self-awareness necessary for effective legal advocacy.

Collaboration and mentoring

Collaboration and mentoring play essential roles in legal education, providing students with valuable opportunities for learning, networking and professional growth. Some ways to expand on this principle are listed below.

Collaborative learning

Encourage collaborative learning opportunities. Emphasize the importance of collaboration and teamwork in legal practice. Assign group projects, case studies and problem-solving exercises that require students to work together to analyse legal issues, develop strategies and propose solutions. Provide guidelines and structure to ensure effective collaboration, such as assigning roles and facilitating group discussions. Encourage students to share their knowledge, skills and perspectives, fostering a sense of collective learning and mutual support.

Peer learning and mentoring

Foster a culture of peer learning by encouraging students to share their knowledge, experiences and insights with one another. Establish mentoring programmes where upper-level students and legal professionals can mentor and support their peers or junior students. These mentoring relationships can provide guidance, advice and networking opportunities, helping students to navigate their legal education and career development. Encourage students to seek out mentors and engage in meaningful mentoring relationships.

Legal professionals as guest speakers

Invite legal professionals from diverse backgrounds to share their experiences and insights with students. Organize guest lectures, panel discussions and networking events where students have the opportunity to interact with professionals in the field. These interactions can provide valuable industry perspectives, expose students to different practice areas and help them to build professional networks. Encourage students to ask questions, seek advice and establish connections with legal professionals.

Internships and work placements

Facilitate opportunities for students to gain practical experience through internships and work placements. Collaborate with law firms, legal organizations and government agencies to provide placements where students can work under the supervision of experienced professionals. These experiences can allow students to apply their legal knowledge in real-world settings, develop practical skills and gain insights into the daily challenges and responsibilities of legal practice.

Networking and professional development

Support students in building their professional networks and developing their professional identities. Organize networking events, career fairs and alumni panels during which students can connect with legal professionals and potential employers. Offer workshops and training sessions on networking skills, CV writing and job interview preparation. Provide resources and guidance on professional development opportunities, such as attending conferences, joining professional organizations and participating in moot court competitions.

Alumni engagement

Foster engagement with alumni, who can serve as mentors, guest speakers and potential employers for students. Establish alumni networks and associations that can facilitate connections between current students and graduates. Encourage alumni to share their experiences and offer guidance to students through mentorship programmes and career advising initiatives. Alumni can also provide valuable insights into career paths, job opportunities and the practical aspects of legal practice.

*

By promoting collaboration and mentoring, legal educators can create an enriching and supportive learning environment in which students can learn from one another and benefit from the wisdom and guidance of legal professionals. These experiences not only enhance students' knowledge and skills but also help them develop important professional relationships and networks that can support their future success in the legal field.

Balancing academic and vocational skills

Balancing academic and vocational skills is crucial in legal education to ensure that students develop a comprehensive skill set that prepares them for the challenges and complexities of legal practice. I set out some ways to expand on this principle below.

An integrated curriculum

Design a curriculum that seamlessly integrates both academic and vocational skills. Incorporate substantive law modules that can provide students with a solid foundation in legal principles, theories and concepts. Simultaneously, infuse practical elements throughout the curriculum to demonstrate the real-world applications of legal knowledge. For example, in a contract law module, students can engage in drafting exercises to apply legal principles to practical scenarios.

Practical skills development

Offer dedicated courses, workshops and modules focused on developing the practical skills necessary for legal practice. These can include legal research and writing, oral advocacy, negotiation, legal drafting and client management. Provide hands-on exercises and simulations that allow students to practise and refine these skills under the guidance of experienced faculty or legal professionals.

Experiential learning opportunities

Provide experiential learning opportunities, such as clinical programmes, work placements and internships, where students can work with clients directly, engage in legal research and writing, and participate in the resolution of real cases. These experiences can allow students to apply their theoretical knowledge in practical settings, developing a deeper understanding of the legal profession and honing their vocational skills in the process.

Case studies and problem-solving exercises

Integrate case studies and problem-solving exercises into the curriculum to bridge the gap between theory and practice. These activities can challenge students to analyse complex legal scenarios, apply legal principles, consider ethical implications and propose solutions. Incorporate practical challenges and dilemmas that lawyers commonly face, encouraging students to develop critical-thinking, reasoning and analytical skills.

Guest lectures and practitioner involvement

Invite legal professionals from diverse practice areas to deliver guest lectures, share their experiences and provide insights into the practical aspects of legal practice. Encourage practitioners to contribute to the curriculum by designing and delivering modules or workshops that focus on the application of legal concepts in real-world contexts. These interactions can expose students to different perspectives, enhance their understanding of the profession, and bridge the gap between academia and practice.

Professional ethics and responsibility

Emphasize the importance of professional ethics, integrity and responsibility throughout the curriculum. Discuss legal ethics and the professional conduct rules and ethical dilemmas faced by lawyers. Encourage students to reflect on their ethical decision making and the impact of their choices on clients, on the legal system and on society as a whole. Incorporate case studies or simulations that present ethical challenges, allowing students to analyse and discuss the ethical implications of different courses of action.

*

By striking a balance between academic and vocational skills, legal educators can equip students with the knowledge, abilities and attitudes necessary for success in the legal profession. This holistic approach ensures that graduates not only possess a solid understanding of legal principles but also have the practical skills, critical-thinking abilities and ethical awareness to navigate the complexities of legal practice and contribute meaningfully to the legal profession.

Continuing professional development

Continuing professional development is crucial for law teachers to stay up to date with the evolving nature of the legal profession and to enhance their teaching effectiveness. Expanding on this principle, some key points to consider are given below.

Training and workshops

Offer regular training sessions, workshops and seminars specifically designed for law teachers to stay updated with current industry trends. These sessions can focus on various aspects, such as legal practice updates, new legal developments, teaching methodologies, assessment strategies and technological advancements in legal education. Collaborate with legal practitioners, industry experts and professional organizations to provide valuable insights and practical knowledge to law teachers.

Conferences and networking

Encourage law teachers to participate in conferences, both national and international, that are relevant to their areas of expertise or teaching interests. These conferences can provide opportunities for professional networking, knowledge exchange and exposure to new teaching approaches and research trends. Support law teachers in presenting their work, sharing their experiences and learning from other educators in the field.

Collaboration with legal practitioners

Foster collaboration between law teachers and legal practitioners to create a bridge between academia and the profession. Invite practitioners as guest speakers or facilitators in classroom discussions, workshops or panel discussions. This collaboration exposes law teachers to real-world legal challenges, practical insights and emerging trends in the legal industry. It also helps foster mutually beneficial relationships between academia and the legal profession.

Reflective practice

Encourage law teachers to engage in reflective practice by regularly taking stock of their teaching methods, thinking about classroom dynamics and listening to student feedback. Provide opportunities for self-assessment and peer observation, where teachers can receive constructive feedback and guidance from their colleagues. This reflective process allows law teachers to identify areas for improvement, explore innovative teaching strategies and refine their pedagogical approaches.

Mentorship and peer learning

Establish mentorship programmes and peer learning communities in which experienced teachers can guide and support their colleagues. Encourage law teachers to engage in collaborative discussions, share best practices and seek advice from their peers. Foster a culture of continuous learning and professional growth within the faculty by creating spaces for collaboration, such as regular meetings, online forums or mentoring circles.

Research and scholarship

Promote research and scholarship among law teachers by providing resources and support for their scholarly endeavours. Encourage law teachers to engage in research projects, publish articles and contribute to the development of legal scholarship. Facilitate access to research grants, library resources and research support services to encourage a culture of scholarly inquiry and intellectual development among the faculty.

*

By prioritizing continuing professional development for law teachers, institutions can ensure that their faculty members are equipped with the necessary knowledge, skills and competencies to provide high-quality legal education. This ongoing training and support not only benefits the individual law teachers but also enhances the overall learning experience for students by exposing them to up-to-date legal knowledge and teaching methodologies that reflect the realities of the legal profession.

SUMMARY OF KEY MESSAGES

The principle of teaching to integrate academic and vocational skills can work in practice

- by designing learning activities that closely mirror real-world legal practice;
- by helping students understand the behaviours and expectations of professional lawyers;
- by recognizing the importance of students' emotions, motivations and experiences in their learning journey;
- by encouraging collaborative learning and mentorship opportunities;
- by integrating both academic and vocational skills throughout the curriculum; and
- by providing continuous training and support to enable law teachers to enhance their own understanding of professional legal practice and stay updated with current industry trends.

By implementing these strategies, law teachers can effectively integrate academic and vocational skills, prepare students for the realities of legal practice, and support their overall professional development.

Addressing the challenges of implementing these strategies requires collaboration among law teachers, curriculum designers, administrators and practitioners. It involves aspects such as ongoing evaluation and refinement of teaching practices, integration of authentic assessment tasks, provision of support and training for law teachers, and a commitment to preparing students with the necessary academic and vocational skills for their future legal careers.

HINTS AND TIPS

» *Relating legal skills teaching to professional behaviour.* Connecting legal skills teaching to the behaviour and practices of professional lawyers through authentic teaching and assessment can be challenging. It requires aligning classroom activities with real-world legal practice and ensuring that students understand the relevance and applicability of what they are learning. Incorporating both traditional academic legal skills (e.g. legal research and reasoning) and vocational skills (e.g. interpersonal skills) into the curriculum in a meaningful way requires careful planning and integration.

» *Integrating the affective domain.* Incorporating the affective domain – including the emotions, motivations and emotional experiences of students – into legal education can be difficult. Engaging with students' affective aspects is crucial for their learning and performance, but it has often been overlooked in legal education. Rethinking curriculum design to embed affect in the curriculum and creating a safe and supportive learning environment requires deliberate effort and strategies such as classroom management, student dialogue and creativity.

» *Developing vocational skills.* The development and integration of vocational skills, such as interpersonal skills, into the legal curriculum can be demanding. While traditional academic legal skills are more familiar and well embedded, the vocational aspect is still under development for many participants. Incorporating authentic assessment tasks and simulations of real legal practice can help bridge the gap between academic and vocational skills, but doing so requires careful planning, resources and support for law teachers, who may lack previous experience in professional practice.

» ***Changing and adapting teaching practices.*** Adapting to new teaching and assessment practices to better prepare students with the skills they will need in their future legal careers can be a challenge. It requires a willingness to change, innovate and continuously improve teaching methods. Providing support and training for law teachers to update their pedagogical approaches and incorporate new practices is essential for successful implementation.

» ***Balancing academic and vocational skills.*** Balancing the integration of academic and vocational skills in the curriculum can be complicated. While traditional academic legal skills are well established, ensuring equal attention is given to vocationally relevant aspects – such as seeking expert advice and understanding parties' interests – requires creating realistic work-based classroom tasks and assessments. Striking the right balance between theoretical knowledge and practical skills can be a complex task.

» ***Demonstrating professional standards and expectations.*** Illustrating professional standards and expectations to students can be hard, especially when it comes to vocational elements. In a professional workplace setting, best practices are often learned through experience and by observing more experienced colleagues. Finding ways to impart these lessons and expectations to students in the law curriculum through simulations and authentic assessment tasks requires careful planning and resources.

Conclusions and recommendations

RESEARCH CONCLUSIONS

This book has focused on the three research questions set out in chapter 3 in order to determine how far-reaching the implementation of practical legal skills teaching in legal curricula has been, the extent to which the most important stakeholders such as law teachers agree, and ultimately what approach this curriculum development has taken. Based on the preceding discussion, tentative conclusions can begin to be drawn. I say 'tentative' because this was a relatively small-scale qualitative study and its findings are therefore not *statistically* generalizable. However, through the detailed study of one particular context it is still possible to clarify relationships, pinpoint critical processes and identify common phenomena,[1] and I believe that these kinds of generalizations are equally valuable. Therefore, despite any potential limitations, to the extent that the findings of this study represent a plausible interpretation of genuine views and behaviour, they allow useful conclusions to be drawn about how authentic assessment and PBL can be used to approach legal skills teaching. Indeed, I would argue that these limitations were in fact key to the design, analysis and findings of my study.

While it may not have involved choosing a representative sample, there is therefore still a firm basis for any claims made as to the value of a qualitative study such as this one so long as the relevant quality criteria for qualitative research are borne in mind. These include credibility of data, dependability of research, transferability of findings and confirmability of conclusions. In this context, any questions about the validity of qualitative research, such as concerns about small sample size and potential bias, can be countered by appropriate methodological rigour, sensitivity to ethical issues and thorough data collection and analysis. All of these aspects were adhered to scrupulously in this study.

Ultimately, the three key research questions for this study – how authentic assessment and PBL have been incorporated into the law curriculum, what the challenges of implementing authentic teaching and assessment practices are, and how these challenges have been overcome in adapting modules and preparing students for employment – are best addressed by reference to the themes discussed in part II of the book. The themes identified through this research – preparing students for professional legal practice; building resilience and improving engagement for widening participation students; teacher and student adaptation to changing environments; responding to challenges of vocational pedagogies; and integrating academic and vocational skills – were then developed as guiding principles that are applicable to authentic assessment and PBL in law schools and that help us gain a better understanding of how law teachers should teach professional legal skills.

In particular, this study seems to suggest that, in fact, although there may be some value in activities that only have certain elements of authentic assessment and PBL, the more authentic the task – in terms of its resemblance to a real-life practical legal scenario – the more valuable it potentially is for developing legal skills in law students, at least from the perspective of law teachers. An important qualification here is the word 'potential', since it also seems clear from this study that student engagement and facilitating self-directed learning are crucial to the incorporation of authentic assessment and PBL, and the absence of either of these elements will have a major impact on the success of these approaches.

At this stage it may be helpful to summarize other unique findings of this research that help enrich the existing literature. Reflecting the increasing importance placed on skills development and employability by the relevant professional and regulatory bodies for UK legal education, the participants in this study made it clear that legal skills, and the issue of how to teach and assess them, has increasingly becoming a focus of their teaching. This study has also shown that the law teachers interviewed are mostly committed to using vocational pedagogies for teaching legal skills in their disciplinary context rather than through decontextualized skills development, and many are working towards overcoming the challenges of implementing these pedagogies.

Furthermore, I found that professional background, in the sense of whether participants had spent time in legal practice as opposed to academia alone, had an impact on their perspectives on teaching professional legal skills, in that there were key differences between them when it came to how this was happening and how authentic assessment and PBL were used to achieve this. This finding highlights the benefit of this study for the purposes of exploring the perspectives of law teachers towards teaching professional legal skills. These perspectives were not previously well known or examined sufficiently.

Another key message seems to be that authentic assessment and PBL can integrate academic and vocational skills into the curriculum, and for this reason they should be more widely used. In particular, when it came to investigating the implementation of legal skills teaching, it was clear from my research that a lot of consideration and action was already taking place in this regard on the part of participants. This was the case even in light of the extremely challenging context of a global pandemic, which in fact accelerated the process of change in some beneficial ways, particularly in relation to the use of technology.

When it comes to better integrating the vocational pedagogies of authentic assessment and PBL into legal curricula, which will be considered in more detail below, relevant innovations can therefore take the form of harnessing and building upon what may well already be taking place in law schools rather than making major disruptive changes and interventions.

RECOMMENDATIONS FOR PROFESSIONAL PRACTICE

In terms of implications for professional practice, a study that identifies how authentic assessment and PBL have been used previously, what their challenges are and the ways of overcoming them has wider significance for approaching legal skills teaching in the future.

Specifically, the PREPS framework provides a set of guiding principles for incorporating authentic assessment and PBL into the law curriculum in order to prepare students for employment, based on the themes of practice, resilience, environment, pedagogy and skills identified in this research.

For example, to help fill gaps in legal education when it comes to performance-based assessment tasks, the teaching for professional practice principle highlighted the benefit of staff without legal practice experience working with those who do have that experience for mutual advantage.

The teaching for resilience and engagement principle recognized the benefits of staff adapting assessments and providing supplemental support for engaging students, particularly those from widening participation backgrounds.

The principle of teaching that adapts to the environment illustrated the importance of improving information and communication technology skills for both law teachers and students, in order to better cope in a changing environment in both the legal education and employment landscapes.

From the teaching to overcome challenges of vocational pedagogies principle it was shown that a diverse and engaging range of formative assessment practices with real-world relevance were essential for enhancing the legal reasoning capabilities of law students.

And finally, the teaching to integrate academic and vocational skills principle demonstrated the need for law teachers to relate authentic teaching and assessment to the behaviour of professional lawyers through a greater focus on vocational skills, in order to help students develop an awareness of appropriate professional practices.

In order to implement the practical recommendations arising out of this study, legal educators should focus on the following specific strategies and approaches.

- The teaching for professional practice principle can be implemented in several ways to enhance the learning experience and prepare law students for professional legal practice, including through authentic assessment, collaborations with professionals, role playing and simulations, clinical programmes and

experiential learning, reflection and feedback, professional skills workshops, integration across the curriculum, and creating a supportive learning environment.
- The teaching for resilience and engagement principle can be implemented in various ways to effectively support students from widening participation backgrounds, including through curriculum design, authentic assessment, collaboration and group work, emotional support and mentorship, tailored feedback and support, employment of engaging teaching methods, community building, continuous reflection and improvement, collaboration with support services, and professional role models.
- Implementing in practice the principle of teaching that adapts to the environment involves incorporating strategies and approaches that enable educators to adjust legal education to changing circumstances, particularly through the use of technology, such as technology integration, experiential learning opportunities, active learning approaches, flexibility and adaptability, authentic assessment, continuous reflection and improvement, and professional development.
- In practice, legal educators can create an engaging and supportive learning environment to implement the principle of teaching to overcome the challenges of vocational pedagogies through various strategies and approaches, including PBL, collaborative learning, formative assessment, authentic assessment tasks, reflection and metacognition, professional skills development, and training and support.
- Implementing the principle of teaching to integrate academic and vocational skills in practical terms involves several strategies to support the overall professional development of students and prepare them for the realities of legal practice, including authentic teaching and assessment, emulating professional behaviour, embedding the affective domain, collaboration and mentoring, balancing academic and vocational skills, and continuing professional development.

Key to the success of any vocational pedagogy seems to be its synthesis with more traditional academic legal pedagogies when integrating the teaching of legal skills into the law curriculum. Although there are some benefits to taking a module-level approach – such as the freedom for law teachers to make individual innovations – a programme-level approach also seems desirable to maintain common standards and more successfully embed the teaching of legal skills into substantive law modules throughout the law curriculum, integrating vocational skills with academic skills in the process.

The findings of this research seem to imply that law teachers do not necessarily tend to see a distinction between vocational and academic legal skills, nor do they see this distinction as useful when it comes to teaching these skills to law students. One potentially useful outcome of this study is that practical solutions have suggested themselves for addressing this dichotomy. Many of the tasks that might seem concerned simply with vocational skills (e.g. oral presentations) are in fact useful – in possessing elements of authentic assessment and PBL – for actually developing the sorts of academic and legal reasoning skills that many law teachers traditionally value as well as being relevant to the real world of practice. These skills include seeing how law interacts with society and serves public policy, understanding that there may be more than one solution to a problem-based scenario, and applying legal principles in practice, then reflecting on them. While such promise has previously been identified in the relevant literature, this study links this potential with empirical data collected from law teachers for the first time. This research therefore goes some way towards examining the views of law teachers in relation to some of the potential benefits of authentic assessment and PBL in law referred to in chapter 2 as having been largely unexplored previously. These benefits include improving student motivation, developing thinking skills and addressing skills gaps in legal education, as well as enhancing employability. This book therefore provides a firm foundation for further research on the benefits of authentic assessment and PBL with a view to making changes to better integrate these benefits into legal curricula.

Notes

PREFACE: INTRODUCTION AND RATIONALE

1. The full thesis can be accessed online at https://discovery.ucl.ac.uk/id/eprint/10139979/.
2. Richard Grimes, Joel Klaff and Colleen Smith. 1996. Legal skills and clinical legal education – a survey of undergraduate law school practice. *The Law Teacher* 30:44–67.
3. Elizabeth Mytton. 2003. Lived experiences of the law teacher. *The Law Teacher* 37:36–54.
4. Geoff Mason. 2009. Employability skills initiatives in higher education: what effects do they have on graduate labour market outcomes? *Education Economics* 17:1–30.
5. Julian Webb and others. 2013. Setting standards: the future of legal services education and training regulation in England and Wales. Report, Legal Education and Training Review (http://letr.org.uk/the-report/index.html).
6. QAA. 2019. *Subject Benchmark Statement: Law.* Quality Assurance Agency for Higher Education (https://www.qaa.ac.uk/docs/qaa/subject-benchmark-statements/subject-benchmark-statement-law.pdf).
7. Aspasia I Tsaoussi. 2020. Using soft skills courses to inspire law teachers: a new methodology for a more humanistic legal education. *The Law Teacher* 54:1–30.
8. Paul Ashwin. 2020. *Transforming University Education: A Manifesto.* Bloomsbury.
9. Ramona Maile Cutri, Juanjo Mena and Erin Feinauer Whiting. 2020. Faculty readiness for online crisis teaching: transitioning to online teaching during the Covid-19 pandemic. *European Journal of Teacher Education* 43:523–541.
10. Francina Cantatore, David McQuoid-Mason, Valeska Geldres-Weiss and Juan Carlos Guajardo-Puga. 2021. A comparative study into legal

education and graduate employability skills in law students through pro bono law clinics. *The Law Teacher* 55:314–336.

CHAPTER 1

1 Mantz Yorke. 2006. *Employability in Higher Education*. York.
2 Paula Baron and Lillian Corbin. 2012. Thinking like a lawyer/acting like a professional: communities of practice as a means of challenging orthodox legal education. *The Law Teacher* 46:100–119.
3 Anne Colby and William M Sullivan. 2008. Formation of professionalism and purpose: perspectives from the preparation for the professions program. *University of St Thomas Law Journal* 5:404–427.
4 Mary Anne Noone and Judith Dickson. 2001. Teaching towards a new professionalism: challenging law students to become ethical lawyers. *Legal Ethics* 4:127–145.
5 Ross Hyams. 2008. On teaching students to 'act like a lawyer': what sort of lawyer? *International Journal of Clinical Legal Education* 13:21–32.
6 David Carless. 2006. Differing perceptions in the feedback process. *Studies in Higher Education* 31:219–233.
7 Michael Eraut and Benedict du Boulay. 2001. Developing the attributes of medical professional judgement and competence. University of Sussex Department of Health (http://users.sussex.ac.uk/~bend/doh/reporthtml.html).
8 George Miller. 1990. The assessment of clinical skills/competence/performance. *Academic Medicine* 65:S63–S67.
9 See annex 6 of the SQE1 pilot assessment specification at www.sra.org.uk/sra/policy/solicitors-qualifying-examination/pilot/sqe-assessment-specification/.
10 Juliet Turner, Alison Bone and Jeanette Ashton. 2018. Reasons why law students should have access to learning law through a skills-based approach. *The Law Teacher* 52:1–16.
11 Peter Knight. 2001. Complexity and curriculum: a process approach to curriculum-making. *Teaching in Higher Education* 6:369–381.
12 Trina Jorre de St Jorre and Beverley Oliver. 2018. Want students to engage? Contextualise graduate learning outcomes and assess for employability. *Higher Education Research and Development* 37:44–57.
13 Paul Ramsden. 2003. *Learning to Teach in Higher Education*, 2nd edn. Routledge.

14 Andrew Litchfield, Jessica Frawley and Skye Nettleton. 2010. Contextualising and integrating into the curriculum the learning and teaching of work-ready professional graduate attributes. *Higher Education Research and Development* 29:519–534.
15 Clair Hughes and Simon Barrie. 2010. Influences on the assessment of graduate attributes in higher education. *Assessment and Evaluation in Higher Education* 35:325–334.
16 Barbara de la Harpe and Christina David. 2012. Major influences on the teaching and assessment of graduate attributes. *Higher Education Research and Development* 31:493–510.
17 Francina Cantatore, David McQuoid-Mason, Valeska Geldres-Weiss and Juan Carlos Guajardo-Puga. 2021. A comparative study into legal education and graduate employability skills in law students through pro bono law clinics. *The Law Teacher* 55:314–336.
18 Jim Cumming. 2010. Contextualised performance: reframing the skills debate in research education. *Studies in Higher Education* 35:405–419.
19 Hughes and Barrie (see note 14).
20 Julian Webb and others. 2013. Setting standards: the future of legal services education and training regulation in England and Wales. Report, Legal Education and Training Review (http://letr.org.uk/the-report/index.html).
21 Anthony Bradney. 2008. Elite values in twenty-first century, United Kingdom law schools. *The Law Teacher* 42:291–301.
22 Jessica Guth and Chris Ashford. 2014. The legal education and training review: regulating socio-legal and liberal legal education? *The Law Teacher* 48:5–19.
23 Maebh Harding. 2016. Using interviewing and negotiation to further critical understanding of family and child law. In *Legal Education: Simulation in Theory and Practice*, ed. C. Strevens, R. Grimes and E. Phillips, p. 128. Routledge.
24 Chloe Wallace. 2010. Using oral assessment in law: opportunities and challenges. *The Law Teacher* 44:365–377.
25 Bill Lucas. 2014. Vocational pedagogy: what it is, why it matters and what we can do about it. Background note for UNESCO–UNEVOC e-Forum, May, p. 2.
26 James Avis. 2014. Workplace learning, VET and vocational pedagogy: the transformation of practice. *Research in Post-Compulsory Education* 19:45–53.

27 Jonny Hall. 2019. Building reflection into the clinic supervision experience: research methods for the reflective teacher. *The Law Teacher* 53:475–486.
28 Morris Keeton and Pamela Tate. 1978. Editors' notes: the boom in experiential learning. In *Learning by Experience: What, Why and How*, ed. M. Keeton and P. Tate, p. 2. Jossey-Bass.
29 Roger Burridge and Julian Webb. 2007. The values of common law legal education: rethinking rules, responsibilities, relationships and roles in the law school. *Legal Ethics* 10:72–97.
30 Ann Hodgson and Ken Spours. 2010. Vocational qualifications and progression to higher education: the case of the 14–19 diplomas in the English system. *Journal of Education and Work* 23:95–110.

CHAPTER 2

1 Cindy Hmelo-Silver. 2004. Problem-based learning: what and how do students learn? *Educational Psychology Review* 16:235–266.
2 Paul Kirschner, John Sweller and Richard Clark. 2006. Why minimal guidance during instruction does not work: an analysis of the failure of constructivist, discovery, problem-based, experiential, and inquiry-based teaching. *Educational Psychologist* 41:75–86.
3 Lesley Hughes and Jeff Lucas. 1997. An evaluation of problem based learning in the multiprofessional education curriculum for the health professions. *Journal of Interprofessional Care* 11:77–88.
4 Janice Herrington, Thomas Reeves and Ron Oliver. 2006. Authentic tasks online: a synergy among learner, task, and technology. *Distance Education* 27:233–247.
5 Andrew Guzzomi, Sally Male and Karol Miller. 2017. Students' responses to authentic assessment designed to develop commitment to performing at their best. *European Journal of Engineering Education* 42:219–240.
6 Noeleen McNamara. 2017. Authentic assessment in contract law: legal drafting. *The Law Teacher* 51:486–498.
7 Caroline Hart, Sara Hammer, Pauline Collins and Toni Chardon. 2011. The real deal: using authentic assessment to promote student engagement in the first and second years of a regional law program. *Legal Education Review* 21:97–121.
8 Henk Schmidt. 1993. Foundations of problem-based learning: some explanatory notes. *Medical Education* 27(5):422–432.

9   Richard Grimes. 2016. Faking it and making it? Using simulation with problem-based learning. In *Legal Education: Simulation in Theory and Practice*, ed. C. Strevens, R. Grimes and E. Phillips. Routledge.
10 Mary Tremblay, Joyce Tryssenaar and Bonny Jung. 2001. Problem-based learning in occupational therapy: why do health professionals choose to tutor? *Medical Teacher* 23:561–566.
11 Carol Boothby and Cath Sylvester. 2017. Getting the fish to see the water: an investigation into students' perceptions of learning writing skills in academic modules and in a final year real client legal clinic module. *The Law Teacher* 51:123–137.
12 See Hart *et al.* (note 7), p. 105.
13 Daniel Berger and Charles Wild. 2017. Enhancing student performance and employability through the use of authentic assessment techniques in extra and co-curricular activities (ECCAs). *The Law Teacher* 51(4):428–439.
14 Kevin Ashford-Rowe, Janice Herrington and Christine Brown. 2014. Establishing the critical elements that determine authentic assessment. *Assessment and Evaluation in Higher Education* 39:205–222.
15 Chloe Wallace. 2010. Using oral assessment in law: opportunities and challenges. *The Law Teacher* 44:365–377.
16 QAA. 2019. *Subject Benchmark Statement: Law*. Quality Assurance Agency for Higher Education (https://www.qaa.ac.uk/docs/qaa/subject-benchmark-statements/subject-benchmark-statement-law.pdf).
17 Madeleine Schultz, Karen Young, Tiffany Gunning and Michelle Harvey. 2021. Defining and measuring authentic assessment: a case study in the context of tertiary science. *Assessment and Evaluation in Higher Education* 47(1):77–94.

CHAPTER 3

1   David Rigg. 2013. Embedding employability in assessment: searching for the balance between academic learning and skills development in law: a case study. *The Law Teacher* 47:404–420.
2   Amanda Coffey and Paul Atkinson. 1996. Concepts and coding. In *Making Sense of Qualitative Data: Complementary Research Strategies (And Social Thought)*, 1st edn, pp. 26–53. Sage.
3   Kathleen Grady and Barbara Wallston. 1988. *Research in Health Care Settings*. Sage.

CHAPTER 4

1   Caroline Hart, Sara Hammer, Pauline Collins and Toni Chardon. 2011. The real deal: using authentic assessment to promote student engagement in the first and second years of a regional law program. *Legal Education Review* 21:97–121.
2   Lucinda Ferguson. 2017. Complicating the 'holy grail', simplifying the search: a critique of the conventional problematisation of social immobility in elite legal education and the profession. *The Law Teacher* 51:377–400.

PART II

1   Aspasia Tsaoussi. 2020. Using soft skills courses to inspire law teachers: a new methodology for a more humanistic legal education. *The Law Teacher* 54:1–30.

CHAPTER 5

1   Lydia Bleasdale and Sarah Humphreys. 2018. Undergraduate resilience research project. Report, University of Leeds (https://teachingexcellence.leeds.ac.uk/wp-content/uploads/sites/89/2018/01/LITEbleasdalehumphreys_fullreport_online.pdf).
2   Rola Ajjawi, Joanna Tai, Tran Le Huu Nghia, David Boud, Liz Johnson and Carol-Joy Patrick. 2020. Aligning assessment with the needs of work-integrated learning: the challenges of authentic assessment in a complex context. *Assessment and Evaluation in Higher Education* 45:304–316.
3   Verónica Villarroel, Susan Bloxham, Daniela Bruna, Carola Bruna and Constanza Herrera-Seda. 2018. Authentic assessment: creating a blueprint for course design. *Assessment and Evaluation in Higher Education* 43:840–854.
4   Freda Grealy. 2018. Experiential training for real-life professional impact: the formation of professional identity in trainee solicitors through a discrete intervention course on ethics and lawyering skills. *The Law Teacher* 52:295–315.
5   SRA. 2020. SQE1 assessment specification. Report (www.sra.org.uk/sra/policy/solicitors-qualifying-examination/sqe1-functioning-legal-knowledge-assessment-specification/#n1).

CHAPTER 6

1. Mitchell Travis. 2016. Teaching professional ethics through popular culture. *The Law Teacher* 50:147–159.
2. Lisa Claydon. 2009. Engaging and motivating students: assessment to aid student learning on a first year core law module. *The Law Teacher* 43:269–283.
3. Caroline Hart, Sara Hammer, Pauline Collins and Toni Chardon. 2011. The real deal: using authentic assessment to promote student engagement in the first and second years of a regional law program. *Legal Education Review* 21:97–121.
4. See Claydon (note 2), p. 282.
5. Kevin Ashford-Rowe, Janice Herrington and Christine Brown. 2014. Establishing the critical elements that determine authentic assessment. *Assessment and Evaluation in Higher Education* 39:205–222.
6. SRA. 2020. SQE1 assessment specification. Report (www.sra.org.uk/sra/policy/solicitors-qualifying-examination/sqe1-functioning-legal-knowledge-assessment-specification/#n1).

CHAPTER 7

1. David Kolb. 1984. *Experiential Learning: Experience as the Source of Learning and Development*. Prentice-Hall.
2. Noelle Higgins, Elaine Dewhurst and Los Watkins. 2012. Field trips as short-term experiential learning activities in legal education. *The Law Teacher* 46:165–178.
3. Craig Newbery-Jones. 2016. Ethical experiments with the D-pad: exploring the potential of video games as a phenomenological tool for experiential legal education. *The Law Teacher* 50:61–81.
4. See Higgins *et al.* (note 2).
5. Practical Law UK: https://uk.practicallaw.thomsonreuters.com/.
6. SRA. 2020. SQE1 assessment specification. Report (www.sra.org.uk/sra/policy/solicitors-qualifying-examination/sqe1-functioning-legal-knowledge-assessment-specification/#n1).

CHAPTER 8

1. Daniel Berger and Charles Wild. 2017. Enhancing student performance and employability through the use of authentic assessment

techniques in extra and co-curricular activities (ECCAs). *The Law Teacher* 51:428–439.
2. Rola Ajjawi, Joanna Tai, Tran Le Huu Nghia, David Boud, Liz Johnson and Carol-Joy Patrick. 2020. Aligning assessment with the needs of work-integrated learning: the challenges of authentic assessment in a complex context. *Assessment and Evaluation in Higher Education* 45:304–316.
3. See Ajjawi *et al.* (note 2), p. 307.
4. David Boud and Elizabeth Molloy. 2013. *Feedback in Higher and Professional Education: Understanding It and Doing It Well*, p. 2. Routledge.
5. Chris Beaumont, Michelle O'Doherty and Lee Shannon. 2011. Reconceptualising assessment feedback: a key to improving student learning? *Studies in Higher Education* 36:671–687.
6. SRA. 2020. SQE1 assessment specification. Report (www.sra.org.uk/sra/policy/solicitors-qualifying-examination/sqe1-functioning-legal-knowledge-assessment-specification/#n1).

CHAPTER 9

1. Aspasia Tsaoussi. 2020. Using soft skills courses to inspire law teachers: a new methodology for a more humanistic legal education. *The Law Teacher* 54:1–30.
2. Rola Ajjawi, Joanna Tai, Tran Le Huu Nghia, David Boud, Liz Johnson and Carol-Joy Patrick. 2020. Aligning assessment with the needs of work-integrated learning: the challenges of authentic assessment in a complex context. *Assessment and Evaluation in Higher Education* 45:304–316.
3. Caroline Maughan. 2011. Why study emotion? In *Affect and Legal Education: Emotion in Learning and Teaching the Law*, ed. P. Maharg and C. Maughan. Routledge.
4. SRA. 2020. SQE1 assessment specification. Report (www.sra.org.uk/sra/policy/solicitors-qualifying-examination/sqe1-functioning-legal-knowledge-assessment-specification/#n1).

CONCLUSIONS AND RECOMMENDATIONS

1. Sarah Delamont and David Hamilton. 1986. Revisiting classroom research: a cautionary tale. In *Controversies in Classroom Research*, ed. M. Hammersley. Open University Press.

Sources

Ajjawi, R., Tai, J., Le Huu Nghia, T., Boud, D., Johnson. L., and Patrick, C.-J. 2020. Aligning assessment with the needs of work-integrated learning: the challenges of authentic assessment in a complex context. *Assessment and Evaluation in Higher Education* 45:304–316.

Ashford-Rowe, K., Herrington, J., and Brown, C. 2014. Establishing the critical elements that determine authentic assessment. *Assessment and Evaluation in Higher Education* 39(2):205–222.

Ashwin, P. 2020. *Transforming University Education: A Manifesto*. Bloomsbury.

Avis, J. 2014. Workplace learning, VET and vocational pedagogy: the transformation of practice. *Research in Post-Compulsory Education* 19(1):45–53.

Baron, P., and Corbin, L. 2012. Thinking like a lawyer/acting like a professional: communities of practice as a means of challenging orthodox legal education. *Law Teacher* 46(2):100–119.

Barrows, H. S., and Tamblyn, R. 1980. *Problem-Based Learning: An Approach to Medical Education*. Springer.

Beaumont, C., O'Doherty, M., and Shannon, L. 2011. Reconceptualising assessment feedback: a key to improving student learning? *Studies in Higher Education* 36(6):671–687.

BERA. 2011. Ethical guidelines for educational research. Report (www.bera.ac.uk/wp-content/uploads/2014/02/BERA-Ethical-Guidelines-2011.pdf).

Berger, D., and Wild, C. 2017. Enhancing student performance and employability through the use of authentic assessment techniques in extra and co-curricular activities (ECCAs). *Law Teacher* 51(4):428–439.

Biggs, J. B. 2003. Constructing learning by aligning teaching: constructive alignment. In *Teaching for Quality Learning at University: What the Student Does*, pp. 11–33. Buckingham: SRHE/Open University Press.

Bleasdale, L., and Humphreys, S. 2018. Undergraduate resilience research project. Report, University of Leeds (https://teachingexcellence.leeds.ac.uk/wp-content/uploads/sites/89/2018/01/LITEbleasdalehumphreys_fullreport_online.pdf).

Boon, A. 2002. Ethics in legal education and training: four reports, three jurisdictions and a prospectus. *Legal Ethics* 5(1):34–67.

Boothby, C., and Sylvester, C. 2017. Getting the fish to see the water: an investigation into students' perceptions of learning writing skills in academic modules and in a final year real client legal clinic module. *Law Teacher* 51(2):123–137.

Boud, D., and Molloy, E. 2013. *Feedback in Higher and Professional Education: Understanding It and Doing It Well*. Routledge.

Bowers-Brown, T. 2006. Widening participation in higher education amongst students from disadvantaged socio-economic groups. *Tertiary Education and Management* 12(1):59–74.

Boyatzis, R. E. 1998. Developing themes and codes. *Transforming Qualitative Information Thematic Analysis and Code Development*, p. 184 (doi: 10.1177/1468794107071408).

Bradney, A. 2008. Elite values in twenty-first century, United Kingdom law schools. *The Law Teacher* 42(3):291–301.

Braun, V., and Clarke, V. 2006. Using thematic analysis in psychology. *Qualitative Research in Psychology* 3(2):77–101.

Brookfield, S. 2001. Through the lens of learning: how the visceral experience of learning reframes teaching. In *Learning, Space and Identity*, C. Paechter *et al.*, pp. 67–77. Sage.

Bryman, A. 2016. *Social Research Methods*, 5th edn. Oxford University Press.

Burgess, H., Sieminski, S., and Arthur, L. 2006. *Achieving Your Doctorate in Education*. Sage.

Burridge, R., and Webb, J. 2007. The values of common law legal education: rethinking rules, responsibilities, relationships and roles in the law school. *Legal Ethics* 10(1):72–97.

Caballero, C. L., and Walker, A. 2010. Work readiness in graduate recruitment and selection: a review of current assessment methods. *Journal of Teaching and Learning for Graduate Employability* 1(1):13–25.

Cantatore, F. et al. 2021. A comparative study into legal education and graduate employability skills in law students through pro bono law clinics. *Law Teacher* 55:314–336.

Carless, D. 2006. Differing perceptions in the feedback process. *Studies in Higher Education* 31(2):219–233 (doi: 10.1080/03075070600572132).

Claydon, L. 2009. Engaging and motivating students: assessment to aid student learning on a first year core law module. *Law Teacher* 43(3):269–283.

Coffey, A., and Atkinson, P. 1996. Concepts and coding. In *Making Sense of Qualitative Data: Complementary Research Strategies (And Social Thought)*, 1st edn, pp. 26–53. Sage.

Colby, A., and Sullivan, W. M. 2008. Formation of professionalism and purpose: perspectives from the preparation for the professions program. *University of St Thomas Law Journal* 5(2):404–427.

Cumming, J. 2010. Contextualised performance: reframing the skills debate in research education. *Studies in Higher Education* 35(4):405–419.

Custer, R. L. et al. 2000. *Using Authentic Assessment in Vocational Education. Information Series No. 381*. Columbus, OH: Office of Educational Research and Improvement.

Cutri, R. M., Mena, J., and Whiting, E. F. 2020. Faculty readiness for online crisis teaching: transitioning to online teaching during the COVID-19 pandemic. *European Journal of Teacher Education* 43(4):523–541.

Dagilyte, E., and Coe, P. 2014. Professionalism in higher education: important not only for lawyers. *Law Teacher* 48(1):33–50.

Delamont, S., and Hamilton, D. 1984. Revisiting classroom research: a continuing cautionary tale. In *Readings on Interaction in the Classroom*, ed. S. Delamont. pp. 3–24. Methuen.

Denscombe, M. 2017. *The Good Research Guide for Small-Scale Social Research Projects*, 6th edn. Open University Press.

Duncan, N. 2015. A future for legal education: personal and professional development and ethics. *Nottingham Law Journal* 24:67–78.

Eraut, M. 1995. Schön shock: a case for reframing reflection-in-action? *Teachers and Teaching* 1(1):9–22.

Eraut, M., and du Boulay, B. 2001. Developing the attributes of medical professional judgement and competence. Report, University of Sussex Department of Health (http://users.sussex.ac.uk/~bend/doh/reporthtml.html).

Evers, M., and Townsley, L. 2017. The importance of ethics in the law curriculum: essential or incidental? *The Law Teacher* 51(1):17–39.

Farran, S. 2013. The 'age of empire': again? *Law Teacher* 47(3):345–367 (doi: 10.1080/03069400.2013.851341).

Feletti, G., and Boud, D. 1997. *The Challenge of Problem-Based Learning*. Kogan Page.

Ferguson, L. 2017. Complicating the 'holy grail', simplifying the search: a critique of the conventional problematisation of social immobility in elite legal education and the profession. *Law Teacher* 51(4):377–400.

Fuller, A., and Unwin, L. 2009. Change and continuity in apprenticeship: the resilience of a model of learning. *Journal of Education and Work* 22(5):405–416.

Gibbs, G. 1988. *Learning by Doing: A Guide to Teaching and Learning Methods*. Oxford: Further Education Unit.

Grady, K. E., and Wallston, B. S. 1988. *Research in Health Care Settings*. Sage.

Grealy, F. 2018. Experiential training for real-life professional impact: the formation of professional identity in trainee solicitors through a discrete intervention course on ethics and lawyering skills. *Law Teacher* 52(3):295–315.

Grimes, R. 2016. Faking it and making it? Using simulation with problem-based learning. In *Legal Education: Simulation in Theory and Practice*, ed. C. Strevens, R. Grimes and E. Phillips. Routledge.

Grimes, R., Klaff, J., and Smith, C. 1996. Legal skills and clinical legal education – a survey of undergraduate law school practice. *Law Teacher* 30(1):44–67.

Guth, J., and Ashford, C. 2014. The legal education and training review: regulating socio-legal and liberal legal education? *Law Teacher* 48(1):5–19.

Guzzomi, A. L., Male, S. A. and Miller, K. 2017. Students' responses to authentic assessment designed to develop commitment to performing at their best. *European Journal of Engineering Education* 42(3):219–240.

Hager, P., and Holland, S. 2006. *Graduate Attributes, Learning and Employability*. Springer.

Hall, J. 2019. Building reflection into the clinic supervision experience: research methods for the reflective teacher. *Law Teacher* 53(4):475–486.

Harding, M. 2016. Using interviewing and negotiation to further critical understanding of family and child law. In *Legal Education: Simulation in Theory and Practice*, ed. C. Strevens, R. Grimes and E. Phillips. Routledge.

Hart, C. *et al.* 2011. The real deal: using authentic assessment to promote student engagement in the first and second years of a regional law program. *Legal Education Review* 21(1):97–121.

Herrington, J., Reeves, T. C., and Oliver, R. 2006. Authentic tasks online: a synergy among learner, task, and technology. *Distance Education* 27(2):233–247.

Higgins, N., Dewhurst, E., and Watkins, L. 2012. Field trips as short-term experiential learning activities in legal education. *Law Teacher* 46(2):165–178.

Hmelo-Silver, C. E. 2004. Problem-based learning: what and how do students learn? *Educational Psychology Review* 16(3):235–266.

Hodgson, A., and Spours, K. 2010. Vocational qualifications and progression to higher education: the case of the 14–19 diplomas in the English system. *Journal of Education and Work* 23(2):95–110.

Hughes, C., and Barrie, S. 2010. Influences on the assessment of graduate attributes in higher education. *Assessment and Evaluation in Higher Education* 35(3):325–334.

Hughes, L., and Lucas, J. 1997. An evaluation of problem based learning in the multiprofessional education curriculum for the health professions. *Journal of Interprofessional Care* 11(1):77–88.

Hyams, R. 2008. On teaching students to 'act like a lawyer': what sort of lawyer? *International Journal of Clinical Legal Education*, 13:21–32.

Iacono, V. L., Symonds, P., and Brown, D. H. K. 2016. Skype as a tool for qualitative research interviews. *Sociological Research Online* 21(2):1–15.

Jones, D. 2019. Legal skills and the SQE: confronting the challenge head on. *Law Teacher* 53(1):35–48.

Jorre de St Jorre, T., and Oliver, B. 2018. Want students to engage? Contextualise graduate learning outcomes and assess for employability. *Higher Education Research and Development* 37(1):44–57.

Keeton, M. T., and Tate, P. J. 1978. Editors' notes: the boom in experiential learning. In *Learning by Experience: What, Why and How*, ed. M. T. Keeton and P. J. Tate, p. 2. San Francisco, CA: Jossey-Bass.

Kember, D. *et al.* 2008. A four-category scheme for coding and assessing the level of reflection in written work. *Assessment and Evaluation in Higher Education* 33(4):369–379.

Killean, R., and Summerville, R. 2020. Creative podcasting as a tool for legal knowledge and skills development. *The Law Teacher* 54(1):31–42.

Kirschner, P. A., Sweller, J., and Clark, R. E. 2006. Why minimal guidance during instruction does not work: an analysis of the failure of constructivist, discovery, problem-based, experiential, and inquiry-based teaching. *Educational Psychologist* 41(2):75–86.

Knight, P., and Page, A. 2007. The assessment of 'wicked' competences. Presentation to the Practice Based Professional Learning Centre for Excellence in Teaching and Learning, Institute of Educational Technology, Open University (https://bit.ly/3KlHgbr).

Knight, P. T. 2001. Complexity and curriculum: a process approach to curriculum-making. *Teaching in Higher Education* 6(3):369–381 (doi: 10.1080/13562510120061223).

Knox, J., and Stone, M. 2019. Embedding employability skills for the legal professionals of the future. *Law Teacher* 53(1):90–101.

Kolb, D. A. 1984. *Experiential Learning: Experience as the Source of Learning and Development*. Englewood Cliffs, NJ: Prentice-Hall.

de la Harpe, B., and David, C. 2012. Major influences on the teaching and assessment of graduate attributes. *Higher Education Research and Development* 31(4):493–510.

Lewinbuk, K. P. 2007. Can successful lawyers think in different languages? Incorporating critical strategies that support learning lawyering skills for the practice of law in a global environment. *The Law Teacher* 41(3):275–286 (doi: 10.1080/03069400.2007.9959748).

Litchfield, A., Frawley, J., and Nettleton, S. 2010. Contextualising and integrating into the curriculum the learning and teaching of work-ready professional graduate attributes. *Higher Education Research and Development* 29(5):519–534.

Loyens, S. M. M., Magda, J., and Rikers, R. M. J. P. 2008. Self-directed learning in problem-based learning and its relationships with self-regulated learning. *Educational Psychology Review* 20(4):411–427.

Lucas, B. 2014. Vocational pedagogy: what it is, why it matters and what we can do about it. Background Note for UNESCO-UNEVOC e-Forum, London.

Lunt, I. 2008. Ethical issues in professional life. In *Exploring Professionalism*, ed. B. Cunningham, 1st edn, pp. 73–98. Institute of Education, University of London.

Madhloom, O. 2019. A normative approach to developing reflective legal practitioners: Kant and clinical legal education. *Law Teacher* 53(4):416–430.

Maharg, P., and Maughan, C. 2011. Introduction. In *Affect and Legal Education: Emotion in Learning and Teaching the Law*, ed. P. Maharg and C. Maughan, pp. 1–10. Routledge.

Malone, S. 2003. Ethics at home: informed consent in your own backyard. *International Journal of Qualitative Studies in Education* 16(6):797–815.

Masole, L., and van Dyk, G. 2016. Factors influencing work readiness of graduates: an exploratory study. *Journal of Psychology in Africa* 26(1):70–73.

Mason, G., Williams, G., and Cranmer, S. 2009. Employability skills initiatives in higher education: what effects do they have on graduate labour market outcomes? *Education Economics* 17(1):1–30.

Mason, J. 2017. *Qualitative Researching*, 3rd edn. Sage.

Maughan, C. 2011. Why study emotion? In *Affect and Legal Education: Emotion in Learning and Teaching the Law*, ed. P. Maharg and C. Maughan, pp. 11–44. Routledge.

McNamara, N. 2017. Authentic assessment in contract law: legal drafting. *Law Teacher* 51(4):486–498.

Miller, G. E. 1990. The assessment of clinical skills/competence/performance. *Academic Medicine* 65(9):563–567.

Moon, J. A. 2004. *Reflection in Learning & Professional Development: Theory & Practice*, 3rd edn. Routledge.

Mytton, E. 2003. Lived experiences of the law teacher. *Law Teacher* 37(1):36–54.

National Committee of Inquiry into Higher Education. 1997. *Higher Education in the Learning Society (Dearing Report)*.

Newbery-Jones, C. 2016. Ethical experiments with the D-pad: exploring the potential of video games as a phenomenological tool for experiential legal education. *Law Teacher* 50(1):61–81.

Nicol, D. J., and Macfarlane-Dick, D. 2006. Formative assessment and self-regulated learning: a model and seven principles of good feedback practice. *Studies in Higher Education* 31(2):199–218.

Noone, M. A., and Dickson, J. 2001. Teaching towards a new professionalism: challenging law students to become ethical lawyers. *Legal Ethics* 4(2):127–145.

O'Toole, J., and Beckett, D. 2013. *Educational Research*, 2nd edn. Oxford University Press.

QAA. 2019. *Subject Benchmark Statement: Law*. Quality Assurance Agency for Higher Education (www.qaa.ac.uk/the-quality-code/subject-benchmark-statements/subject-benchmark-statement-law).

Ramsden, P. 2003. *Learning to Teach in Higher Education*, 2nd edn. Routledge.

Redmond, P. 2006. Outcasts on the inside: graduates, employability and widening participation. *Tertiary Education and Management* 12(2):119–135.

Rigg, D. 2013. Embedding employability in assessment: searching for the balance between academic learning and skills development in law: a case study. *Law Teacher* 47(3):404–420.

Robson, C. 2011. *Real World Research*, 3rd edn. Wiley.

Rowe, M., Murray, M., and Westwood, F. 2012. Professionalism in pre-practice legal education: an insight into the universal nature of professionalism and the development of professional identity. *Law Teacher* 46(2):120–131.

Ryan, P. 2017. Teaching collaborative problem-solving skills to law students. *Law Teacher* 51(2):138–150.

Schmidt, H. G. 1993. Foundations of problem-based learning: some explanatory notes. *Medical Education* 27(5):422–432.

Schmidt, H. G., Rotgans, J. I., and Yew, E. H. J. 2011. The process of problem-based learning: what works and why. *Medical Education* 45(8):792–806.

Schneider, A. K. 2012. Teaching a new negotiation skills paradigm. *Washington University Journal of Law & Policy* 39:13–38.

Schön, D. 1995. Educating the reflective legal practitioner. *Clinical Law Review* 2:231–250.

Schultz, M. *et al.* 2021. Defining and measuring authentic assessment: a case study in the context of tertiary science. *Assessment and Evaluation in Higher Education* 47(1):1–18.

Seale, C. 1999. *The Quality of Qualitative Research*. Sage.

Sherr, A. 1998. Legal education, legal competence and Little Bo Peep. *Law Teacher* 32(1):37–63.

SRA. 2015. Statement of solicitor competence (www.sra.org.uk/solicitors/resources/cpd/competence-statement/).

SRA. 2020. SQE1 assessment specification (www.sra.org.uk/sra/policy/solicitors-qualifying-examination/sqe1-functioning-legal-knowledge-assessment-specification/#n1).

Strevens, C., Grimes, R., and Phillips, E. 2016. *Legal Education: Simulation in Theory and Practice*. Routledge.

Thomas, L., and May, H. 2010. *Inclusive Learning in Higher Education*. Higher Education Academy.

Tomlinson, M. 2008. 'The degree is not enough': students' perceptions of the role of higher education credentials for graduate work and employability. *British Journal of Sociology of Education* 29(1):49–61.

Travis, M. 2016. Teaching professional ethics through popular culture. *The Law Teacher* 50(2):147–159.

Tremblay, M., Tryssenaar, J., and Jung, B. 2001. Problem-based learning in occupational therapy: why do health professionals choose to tutor? *Medical Teacher* 23(6):561–566.

Tsaoussi, A. I. 2020. Using soft skills courses to inspire law teachers: a new methodology for a more humanistic legal education. *The Law Teacher* 54(1):1–30.

Turner, J., Bone, A., and Ashton, J. 2018. Reasons why law students should have access to learning law through a skills-based approach. *Law Teacher* 52(1):1–16.

Villarroel, V. *et al.* 2018. Authentic assessment: creating a blueprint for course design. *Assessment and Evaluation in Higher Education* 43(5):840–854.

Wallace, C. J. 2010. Using oral assessment in law: opportunities and challenges. *Law Teacher* 44(3):365–377.

Waters, B. 2013. Widening participation in higher education: the legacy for legal education. *The Law Teacher* 47(2):261–269.

Webb, J. *et al.* 2013. Setting standards: the future of legal services education and training regulation in England and Wales (http://letr.org.uk/the-report/index.html).

Yorke, M. 2006. Employability in higher education. Report, Advance HE (www.advance-he.ac.uk/knowledge-hub/employability-higher-education-what-it-what-it-not).

Zepke, N., Nugent, D., and Leach, L. 2003. *Reflection to Transformation: A Self-Help Book for Teachers*. Dunmore Press.